Restoring a Nation
of Home Owners

Restoring a Nation of Home Owners

What went wrong with home ownership in Britain, and how to start putting it right

Peter Saunders

CIVITAS

First Published June 2016

© Civitas 2016
55 Tufton Street
London SW1P 3QL

email: books@civitas.org.uk

ISBN 978-1-906837-80-8

Independence: Civitas: Institute for the Study of Civil Society is a registered educational charity (No. 1085494) and a company limited by guarantee (No. 04023541). Civitas is financed from a variety of private sources to avoid over-reliance on any single or small group of donors.

All publications are independently refereed. All the Institute's publications seek to further its objective of promoting the advancement of learning. The views expressed are those of the authors, not of the Institute, as is responsibility for data and content.

Designed and typeset by
lukejefford.com

Printed in Great Britain by
4edge Limited, Essex

Contents

Author   vi

Acknowledgements   vii

Executive Summary   viii

1. The end of the home owner revolution?   1

2. Do people still want to own?   14

3. The bubble that never burst   20

4. Is tight supply the main problem?   39

5. New sources of demand   65

6. How government policy
   is making matters worse   82

7. Some modest proposals   98

Notes   120

Author

Peter Saunders was an academic in Britain before spending 10 years in Australian think tanks. He is now back in Britain and semi-retired. He is a Professorial Research Fellow at Civitas, a Professor Emeritus at the University of Sussex, and a Distinguished Fellow of the Centre for Independent Studies in Sydney. His previous Civitas publications include *Social Mobility Myths* (2010), *The Rise of the Equalities Industry* (2011) and *Beyond Beveridge* (2013). His work over the years has focused on welfare reform, social mobility, income inequality and poverty, as well as housing and home ownership. In this new book, he returns to issues of fairness and affordability he first addressed in *A Nation of Home Owners*, published back in 1990.

Acknowledgements

The author wishes to thank Daniel Bentley, Kristian Niemietz, Sundran Rajendra and Peter Williams for their invaluable comments, criticisms and suggestions on an earlier draft of this essay. It goes without saying that they bear no responsibility for any errors and weaknesses that remain, and that the views and arguments expressed in the text are those of the author alone.

Executive Summary

After almost a century of continuous expansion, the rate of home ownership in Britain has fallen from 70 per cent of households in 2000 to fewer than 65 per cent today. Among the under-forties it has dipped alarmingly. This book asks what has caused this decline in home ownership, why it matters, and what might be done to reverse it.

The spread of home ownership in the twentieth century has distributed ownership of wealth more widely than ever before. It has also strengthened ties of community and rates of civic participation. Mass owner-occupation has in these ways benefited individuals and the wider society.

The decline of home ownership since 2000 does not reflect any significant change in people's housing preferences. Surveys find that the great majority of people in all age groups would still prefer to own, but increasing numbers can no longer afford to buy. Many under-forties, in particular, have been shut out of home ownership by rising prices and the demand for huge deposits on housing loans.

House prices in Britain have been rising faster than the general rate of inflation for more than 50 years, and this has created significant capital gains for several generations of owners. But until the late 1990s, these gains did not come at the expense of new generations of buyers because average house prices and average earnings increased at similar rates. So although the *price* of houses rose relative to other commodity prices, the *cost* of housing remained constant relative to what people were earning. Existing owners made gains, but houses remained no more expensive for new generations to buy than they had been for their parents.

This link between average house prices and average earnings has now been broken. There have been four big house price booms in Britain since 1970. In the first three (1971-73, 1977-79 and 1987-89) house prices soon fell back into line with earnings. But in the fourth boom, which began in the late nineties, this never happened. Between 2000 and 2014, average earnings rose by 51 per cent, but average house prices rose by 132 per cent. The result is that the younger generation is now expected to pay a much bigger multiple of its earnings to buy a home than its parents did – something that never happened previously. The baby boomers are now making capital gains at the expense of their children.

Some young people can still afford to pay these much higher prices because interest rates have been at historically low levels since the 2008 global financial crisis. But new buyers are taking out huge loans to purchase property which is 20 or 30 per cent over value. With inflation so low, these loans will take many years to clear and will become crippling if and when interest rates return to normal levels. Meanwhile, new lending rules since 2008 require huge deposits which few borrowers can provide without assistance from family, the government, or both.

Many experts believe that this unprecedented and deeply damaging 'fourth house price boom' has been caused mainly by our failure to build enough houses.

They blame this on land hoarding by developers, greedy landowners, and conservative planning authorities which respond to pressure from local residents by refusing development permits.

There are, however, strong reasons for arguing that restricted supply was not the key cause of this crisis of housing affordability, and that even if we increased construction as many have urged, the impact on house prices would be small. Over the last 40 years, housing supply has increased faster than the growth in the number of households, so scarcity is no worse now than it was in the 1970s. Fluctuations in housing supply have not been reflected in changes in price levels and countries like Ireland, which built many new homes, suffered worse house price inflation than Britain did. Economic modelling commissioned by the government predicts that even if we expanded the current rate of building by 50 per cent per year for the next 15 years, real house prices would hardly fall at all.

The main causes of our problem have been on the demand side. The failure to control the explosion of credit from the late 1990s onwards grossly inflated house prices, and the historically low cost of credit since 2008 has kept them inflated and prevented the price correction which is necessary to restore the link with earnings (as occurred in the three previous house price booms). The growth of buy-to-let has further fuelled demand, and this has been reinforced by an influx of foreign money into the luxury London market, the strong growth in immigrant numbers, and an increase in the number of parents' drawing down their own housing equity to help their children buy.

Recent government attempts to resolve the affordability problem by subsidising buyers have only thrown fuel on the flames. Help to Buy equity loans and mortgage guarantees have almost certainly pushed prices even higher, and new pension freedoms have channelled more new money into housing. Demand-side subsidies should be wound up as the first step to restoring affordability.

Two other key proposals are advanced. The first is that the Bank of England should be given a statutory duty to regulate mortgage lending to keep the ratio of average house prices to average earnings within a specified range over the medium term. We must never again allow a house price boom to get out of control and go uncorrected as has happened since the late 1990s.

Secondly, in order to rectify the existing generational inequality in access to home ownership, the Right to Buy (RTB), which is currently enjoyed by tenants in the social rented sector, should be extended to tenants of landlords in the private sector with discounts capped to prevent landlords incurring losses. This RTB should not apply to properties less than 25 years old, landlords should be partially compensated by capital gains tax concessions when they sell, and the standard duration of tenancies in the private sector should be extended to five years.

1

The end of the home owner revolution?

In 1990 I published a book about one of the most important social changes to have taken place in Britain in the twentieth century: the growth of mass home ownership. Echoing Napoleon's jibe about Britain being a nation of shopkeepers, I called the book *A Nation of Home Owners*.[1] The title celebrated the fact that two-thirds of British households were by then owners of their own homes, and their numbers seemed certain to keep growing.

Quarter of a century later, home ownership in Britain has gone into decline. The proportion of households owning their homes has dropped by five percentage points since the turn of the century, and most experts expect it to fall further. The owner-occupation rate among younger households has dropped alarmingly. In 2001, 60 per cent of 25-34 year olds owned their homes; today it is just over 40 per cent.[2] The HomeOwners' Alliance, a lobby group campaigning on behalf of owner-occupiers, has warned: 'We are unwittingly sleepwalking back to becoming a nation of renters.'[3]

In this new book, I try to answer three basic questions. First, what has caused this decline in home ownership? Secondly, does it matter? And thirdly, what, if anything, might we do to reverse it? We start with some history.

The spread of home ownership in the twentieth century

Before the First World War, few families in Britain could dream of owning the homes they lived in. In the Edwardian era, it has long been thought that as few as 10 per cent of households owned, although recent estimates put the figure higher at 23 per cent.[4] What is not disputed is that the great majority of people did not own their homes but rented from private landlords (for there was almost no state rental housing at that time).

But in the inter-war years, a dramatic change started to occur. The break-up of the great estates after World War I released a lot of new land, and improved transport links (together with the spread of car ownership) opened up the commuter belt around London and other major cities. Private builders started producing good quality homes on cheap land, and middle class families started buying them to live in. By the outbreak of World War II, almost one-third of British households owned their homes outright or on mortgage, and home ownership among the middle classes had become the norm.

After a brief lull immediately after the war, when building materials for private sector construction were tightly rationed, the home ownership revolution picked up again in the fifties and sixties. And this time, many 'respectable' working class families joined in.

Private builders continued to produce high volumes of affordable new housing in the expanding suburbs, and in addition, many working class renters were given the opportunity to buy their homes from their landlords at knock-down prices. A combination of rent controls (introduced by the wartime government in 1915 as a 'temporary measure', but never lifted until the Thatcher years) and tight security of tenure laws had made it increasingly difficult for private landlords to get a reasonable return on their capital, so many disinvested, selling cheaply to their sitting tenants. By 1971 (the first year that housing tenure was measured in the census), half the country was in owner-occupation.

The third and final stage of the home owner revolution started in 1979, when Margaret Thatcher offered council tenants the right to buy their homes from local councils at substantial discounts. This opened up home ownership to even more working class families, and many grabbed the opportunity. Their votes helped sweep the Conservatives into office.

Since 1980, as many as two million council homes have been sold.[5] Most sales took place in the Thatcher years and involved houses on the more desirable estates (tenants were less inclined to buy flats on problem estates, even though the government raised the discounts for flats in 1986).[6] Council house sales helped push the UK home ownership rate up by as much as 10 percentage points after 1980.[7]

A social revolution

When I wrote my book, almost two-thirds of British households were home owners, and 90 per cent said they would like to buy. It seemed that a 'social revolution' had transformed British society, economically, politically and culturally.

1. A wider distribution of wealth

Economically, the expansion of home ownership spread the ownership of wealth across the social classes. For the first time in our history, it became normal in Britain for ordinary people to own significant property assets.[8]

Wealth is, of course, still very unequally distributed in Britain (it is much more unequally distributed than incomes). Nevertheless, many 'ordinary people' now own assets of significant value. The median British household in 2012 owned assets worth £218,400, and although a quarter of (mainly younger) households owned less than £57,000, the richest quarter (who were mainly older) owned more than £490,900. Even households in the bottom fifth of incomes (total annual household income less than £15,800) enjoyed a median total wealth of £63,700.[9]

The two principal components of most people's wealth holdings are their pension pots and their homes. Both expanded significantly in Britain in the twentieth century, with the result that wealth came to be spread among many more people than previously. In countries where home ownership did not expand to the same extent, wealth inequality has tended to remain more marked than in Britain (even if their income distribution is more equal). Latest OECD estimates find, for example, that Germany (where home ownership has always been much lower than in Britain) is among the least equal countries as regards wealth distribution, while Britain ranks among the more equal. The share of national wealth held by the richest 10 per cent in Britain is significantly below the OECD average and is lower than in France, Norway, Germany, or the Netherlands.[10]

Not only has the expansion of home ownership in Britain helped spread ownership of wealth, but housing has turned out to be a high-performing asset which for most people in most periods since the war has generated a substantial and real rate of return on their initial capital outlay.[11] As we shall see in chapter 3, house prices have tended to rise faster than the average rate of inflation, which means that owning your own home has been a significant means of accumulating wealth. The more house prices have risen, the greater the capital gains that home owners have been able to accrue.

Of course, most people only own one house – the home they live in – and the capital gains they accumulate may therefore appear notional. If they sell up to get their hands on the money, they will have to plough the proceeds back into another purchase, which means they end up no better off. However, these capital gains are often realised in part or in whole as people grow older.

Once the mortgage is paid off, owners live rent-free (while the housing costs of tenants keep inflating throughout their lifetimes as rents rise). Owners enjoy what economists call an 'imputed rental income' from their houses, and this boosts their effective, real incomes later in life. Governments used to tax this imputed 'income' under Schedule 'A' (income from property), but this was scrapped in the early 1960s.[12]

Furthermore, when the kids leave home, owners can 'trade down' to a smaller house and realise part of the capital gain embodied in the bricks and mortar. This can fund foreign holidays, cruises, the classic sports car they always promised themselves – and/or it enables them to give their children or grandchildren a kick-start, funding school fees or paying for the deposit on a house for them.

Most crucially of all, provided the capital hasn't been leeched away in nursing home fees at the end of life,[13] the asset value accumulated by an owner-occupier can be left to their heirs, to start a mini-dynasty. For the first time in our history, ordinary people now expect to bequeath significant sums of wealth to their successors and to inherit significant sums from their predecessors. As I noted back in 1990:

> The present generation of owners will not simply leave a lot of money to its children, but many of them will themselves inherit substantial sums from their parents... each generation from here on will benefit from its parents while in turn benefiting its children. The seed corn planted from the 1930s onwards is now being harvested, and the next generation of fruit has already been sown.[14]

If you want to know about economic inequality today, you need to look not only at the incomes people are earning, but at the housing wealth that is gradually passing through successive generations of their family.

2. A new political force

A second dimension of the twentieth century home owner revolution has been its impact on politics.

Analysts are uncertain how much difference housing tenure makes to how people vote, although there is little doubt that the Right to Buy helped win the Tories working class votes in 1979 and 1983. At the 1983 election, 56 per cent of council house buyers voted Conservative and 59 per cent of former Labour voters who had bought their homes switched to the Tories.[15]

More than 30 years later, David Cameron's Conservatives offered a similar Right to Buy deal to 1.3 million tenants of housing associations. The jury is still out on whether or not this policy helped them at the 2015 election,[16] but it certainly won't have lost them any votes. The calculation that it would win votes was a major factor in the Conservatives' decision to include the promise in their manifesto.

Home owners not only make up a majority of the electorate – they are also much more likely to vote than tenants. At the 2010 General Election, 74 per cent of outright owners voted, as did 67 per cent of owners with mortgages, but turnout among tenants was down at 55 per cent.[17]

And the political clout of home owners goes far beyond mere voting. Home owners often constitute a clear and well-organised interest group at local level (particularly with regard to planning controversies), and to some extent at national level too.[18] Precisely because so many owners expect to accumulate so much capital through their houses, they can be very sensitive about any political threats to their property values. Politicians certainly believe this and behave accordingly.

At local level, home owner opposition to new housing developments (so-called 'NIMBYism') can be a major factor in restricting the supply of new housing and thereby protecting existing high property values in an area. We shall discuss this further in chapter 4.

At national level too, governments of all parties have found it expedient to maintain and extend tax concessions to home owners. We have already encountered one example of this, the abolition of Schedule A tax on the imputed rental incomes of owner-occupiers. Although mortgage interest tax relief (the obverse side of Schedule A)[19] was eventually phased out too, home owners continue to enjoy favoured tax status in other areas. When capital gains tax was introduced in 1965, for example, the family home was exempted and it has remained exempt ever since.

Access to many means-tested welfare benefits also often exempts housing assets (although this is not the case for state assistance with residential aged care).

Recently, taxes levied on housing inheritance were relaxed to curry favour with elderly home owners who want to pass their property onto their children. In 2007, George Osborne, then Conservative shadow chancellor, promised if elected to raise the inheritance tax threshold to £1 million, and this created such a surge in Tory support that Prime Minister Gordon Brown postponed a general election which he'd seemed poised to call and win. Eight years later, in his first budget governing without the need for Liberal Democrat support, Osborne delivered on this promise with a new 'Family Homes Allowance'. From 2017, the first half a million pounds (for individuals) or million pounds (for couples) of housing wealth will be exempt from inheritance tax. This measure will cost over £1 billion in lost revenue, and the shortfall will be made up by higher taxes on pension contributions by those earning in excess of £150,000p.a.[20]

Sociologists often point to the power and influence of an 'elite class' of high-earning professionals, business leaders and financiers.[21] Yet it was this class that lost out when the government agreed to scrap inheritance tax on modestly-priced homes and to increase taxes on the pension contributions of the highest earners instead. Make no mistake: the home-owning 'middle mass' has real political clout.

3. A culture of independence

The third element in the home owner revolution has been cultural. The spread of home ownership has strengthened core values emphasising personal autonomy, privacy, family security and independence from interference by the state. These are all values that would be cherished by any nineteenth century classical liberal.

Successive generations of politicians (Labour as well as Conservative) have claimed that there is something 'natural' about the desire to own one's own home. In 1951, Harold Macmillan spoke of home ownership fulfilling a 'deep desire in [people's] hearts'; a 1971 Conservative government white paper identified a 'deep and natural desire on the part of the householder to have independent control of the house that shelters him and his family'; a 1977 Labour government housing policy review suggested that 'owning one's home is a basic and natural desire' and that owner-occupation 'satisfies deep-seated aspirations'; in 1985, Margaret Thatcher declared that 'the desire to have and to hold something of one's own is basic to the spirit of man';[22] and in 2015, David Cameron celebrated 'owning your own home' as 'the most natural instinct in the world'.[23]

Taken literally, we cannot have evolved a 'natural instinct' to own rather than rent, but it is possible that home ownership taps into some deep human instincts. In *A Nation of Home Owners*, I found little evidence that we are naturally territorial, but we do exhibit a strong possessive instinct – a natural disposition to hold what we have and exclude strangers from sharing it.[24] In modern societies, this gets expressed in the strong desire to own personal property, especially housing.

Many owners talk of the sense of independence and control which home ownership has given them. They refer to the 'pride' that ownership brings; the sense of personal achievement it entails; the 'feeling of freedom' they get by being able to do what they want in their own place; the comfort they derive from knowing that nobody can take it away from them. Asked to name the principal advantages of owning rather than renting a house, the top six answers are: autonomy (the freedom to do what you want); capital appreciation; avoiding the 'waste' of perpetual rental payments; security of tenure; pride of ownership; and the ability to pass on a legacy to one's children.[25]

Owners are more likely than tenants to invest a sense of identity in their houses (64 per cent of the owners in my research felt strong feelings of attachment to their homes, compared with only 40 per cent of council tenants). They spend more time working in and on their houses (and generally deriving a sense of satisfaction from the results). And they are often more engaged with their immediate neighbours and local communities.

It has often been claimed that home ownership 'privatises' and 'individualises' people, disengaging them from the wider society and eroding 'social capital'.[26] Socialist intellectuals have commonly distrusted home ownership precisely because they think it breaks down class solidarity (workers are too busy papering the parlour to get out in the streets and make revolution with their neighbours). But my research among home owners and council tenants in Slough, Derby and Burnley found that (even after controlling for income differences), home owners were five times more likely to belong to local residents' organisations, and were twice as likely to belong to a trade union. More recently, an OECD review of the evidence confirms that, 'Homeownership tends to be associated with more active and informed citizens and more residentially stable neighbourhoods.'[27]

The revolution hits the buffers

It has been 25 years since *A Nation of Home Owners* was published, and most of the claims I made in that book still stand up reasonably well. Home ownership is still the preferred tenure of the vast majority of UK households; people continue to make substantial capital gains as a result of owning a house; home owners continue to represent a significant political force; and the psychic and social benefits of owning one's home remain strong. One thing, however, has changed dramatically: home ownership is no longer expanding. Indeed, since the turn of the century, it has started to shrink.

Figure 1 charts the proportion of households owning and renting their homes (either from private landlords, or from local councils and housing associations) since 1914. It shows how home ownership and social renting both expanded at the expense of private renting up until the 1980s. But it also shows that, since the 1980s, there have been significant changes in all three major tenures.

The size of the social rented sector has almost halved in this period. Its composition has also radically changed as councils have been displaced as landlords by housing associations. In 1981, one-third of British households were in social rented housing, and all but six per cent of them were in council-owned accommodation. Since then, the proportion of social renters has fallen to just 18 per cent of households (fewer than the number of private tenants for the first time since the 1960s), and more than half of them now rent from housing associations, not local authorities. Council house sales bit a large chunk out of this sector in the 1980s and 1990s (when its size fell from 33 per cent to 21 per cent); reduced rates of building account for the rest of the fall.

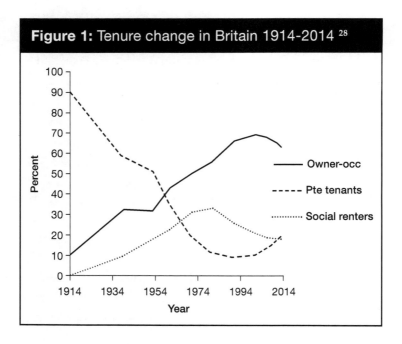

Figure 1: Tenure change in Britain 1914-2014 [28]

In the private rented sector, the story is very different, for the long collapse through most of the twentieth century has been reversed. The abolition of rent controls and the introduction of assured shorthold tenancies in the Housing Acts of 1980 and 1988 meant that landlords could once again invest in housing and make a profit (housing benefit now makes up the difference between market rents and what low-income tenants can afford to pay).[29] The sector responded slowly at first, growing just one percentage point (from nine to 10 per cent) between 1991 and 2001. But since the turn of the century, its growth has accelerated with extraordinary pace as hundreds of thousands of small investors[30] have taken advantage of buy-to-let mortgages to buy houses. As a result, today 19 per cent of British households are renting from private landlords – the highest figure since 1971.

The growth of home ownership, however, has hit the buffers in the last 15 years. Owner-occupation rates continued to rise until the turn of the century, peaking at almost 70 per cent of households, but since then, for the first time in our modern history, they have begun to fall.[31] By 2013 home ownership had dipped back below 65 per cent, the lowest level since the 1980s, and the UK owner-occupancy rate had fallen to one of the lowest in the developed world. Most pundits expect it to fall further in the future.[32]

Table 1: Home ownership rates in selected EU and 'Anglosphere' countries, 2013 [33]	
Hungary	90 per cent
Poland	84 per cent
Czech Republic	80 per cent
Spain	78 per cent
Greece	76 per cent
Portugal	74 per cent
Italy	73 per cent
Belgium	72 per cent
Ireland	70 per cent
Sweden	70 per cent
Canada	68 per cent
Netherlands	67 per cent
Australia	67 per cent
New Zealand	65 per cent
USA	65 per cent
UK	65 per cent
France	64 per cent
Denmark	63 per cent
Germany	53 per cent

The question is: why? What happened in the last 15 years that stopped the home owner revolution dead in its tracks, and then, against all expectations, began to reverse it?

2

Do people still want to own?

If we want to explain why owner-occupation has gone into decline, the obvious first question to ask is: do people still want to own their homes?

It appears that, overwhelmingly, they do. The 2010 British Social Attitudes Survey (BSAS)[1] found that 86 per cent of people aged over 18 in England said that, given a free choice, they would prefer to buy rather than rent their home. Owner-occupation was the preferred choice of 95 per cent of existing owners, but also of around 60 per cent of council and housing association tenants.

Far from declining in popularity, the BSAS shows that owner-occupation has become significantly *more* popular than it used to be. In the 1980s, surveys found only around three-quarters of people preferring to own.[2] The preference for home ownership has therefore strengthened by about 10 percentage points over the last 30 years.

Satisfaction with home ownership among those who have achieved it also remains high. In a 2009 survey, only two per cent of owners were dissatisfied with their accommodation, compared with 10 per cent of private tenants and 13 per cent of council or housing association tenants.[3] The 2010 BSAS survey found the main reasons for preferring ownership were that it is a good investment, it offers greater security, and it allows people to do what they want with their property. These are much the same answers as I recorded in my interviews with owner-occupiers and council tenants back in 1986.

But what of generational differences? Young people today are 'settling down' later than they used to. Many more attend university or undergo further education or training than in the past, which means they are starting their careers later than ever before. Young people are also leaving home later; they are committing to marriage or long-term partnerships later; and they are having children later.[4] All of this might lead people in their twenties and thirties to express less interest in buying a house or flat than used to be the case. They won't want to buy until they are ready to settle down.

Many young people are also burdened with debt as a result of taking on loans for higher education courses – something older generations never faced. This might have put them off the idea of buying a house with a huge mortgage. And the anti-capitalist movement in the early years of this century, reinforced by the fall-out from the 2008 financial crash, might have triggered a culture shift against the whole idea of private property ownership.[5] If this were the case, we would expect to find younger people expressing less interest in owning a house, not only in the foreseeable future, but at any time in their lives.

Interestingly, the BSAS finds no significant differences in the tenure preferences expressed by different age groups – young people are just as keen on owning as older ones. But this has been contradicted by other studies.

A 2010 review by the Joseph Rowntree Foundation found that the under-25s were becoming markedly less keen on home ownership, at least in the short-term.[6] Back in 1990, 70 per cent of 18-25 year olds said they would like to own in the next two years, but this figure dropped to below 40 per cent by 2003, and was still below 50 per cent in 2007, just before the big financial crash. These results could reflect the delayed maturity of younger people today, but there was also some sign that the 25-34 year olds were cooling off as well. If this is the case, we could be looking at a more sustained decline in the desire to own.

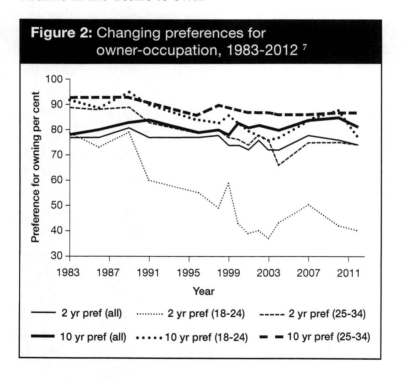

Figure 2: Changing preferences for owner-occupation, 1983-2012 [7]

The Council of Mortgage Lenders says it's too early to tell: 'We will not know for many years whether the British love affair with home ownership is cooling.'[8]

Like the Joseph Rowntree Foundation, the CML finds that the desire to own in two years' time has fallen over the last 30 years among the under-25s, and to a lesser extent in the 25-34 age group as well (Figure 2). In the 1980s, between 70 and 80 per cent of under-25s wanted to own within two years, but since 2000 the proportion has been hovering around 40 per cent (this large fall shows up clearly in the graph). Almost nine out of 10 of those aged 25-34 in the 1980s said they'd like to own within two years, but in recent years this has been closer to three-quarters. No such decline is found in the older age groups. These figures support the idea that young people are settling down later and are therefore less keen on buying at a relatively early age than their parents and grandparents were.

However, the CML also asked respondents for their preferred tenure in 10 years' time. This gives a better idea of whether or not people are going off the very idea of owning. In the population as a whole, the preference for owning in 10 years' time rose from around 60 per cent in the 1970s to around 80 per cent in the 1980s, and that, more or less, is where it has stayed. It fell from 85 per cent in 2010 to 81 per cent in 2012, and the CML thinks this might indicate a 'loss of appetite for home ownership', but this is tenuous. The 2010 figure was the highest ever recorded, and as Figure 2 shows (the heavy solid line), the figures have been fluctuating up and down by a few percentage points for quite a few years without revealing any clear trend (the proportion preferring ownership stood at only 80 per cent in 2004, for example).

More interesting is the trend in ten-year tenure preferences among the younger age groups. In the 1980s, more than 90 per cent of the under-25s said they'd like to own in the next ten years, and similar figures were recorded for those aged 25-34. In the 1990s, the enthusiasm of both groups dipped a bit (fluctuating around the 85 per cent mark for the under-25s and around the high-80s for the 25-34s). Since 2000, the 25-34 group has remained in the high 80s, but the under-25s have slipped a bit further and now register mainly in the high 70s. All of this would seem to suggest that younger people have over the last 30 years become slightly less interested in the dream of one day buying a home, although the shift is not great.

This interpretation is supported by the Halifax 'Generation Rent' survey of 2015. This focuses on people aged between 20 and 45, and it claims to detect 'the emergence of a new demographic split between those who want to get on the housing ladder and those who say they don't.'[9] Over the last five years, home ownership in this age group has fallen slightly, from 46 to 45 per cent, while the proportion of those saying they do not want to own has risen from 13 to 16 per cent – a significant rise in disenchantment.

There is no evidence from any of these surveys of a marked sea-change in tenure preferences in Britain over the last 20 years or so (and compared with 40 years ago, we are still much keener). The great majority of people in all age groups would still prefer to own, if not now, then at some point in the future.

But it does seem from all this evidence that younger cohorts may have started to become slightly disillusioned with home ownership. It is not so much that they don't ever want it; more that increasingly, they don't believe they will ever achieve it. Our aspirations tend to be trimmed over time to fit our expectations, for there is no point in continuing to hanker after the impossible.

Better than making yourself miserable is to adjust your preferences so they are more realistic.[10]

The Halifax survey found that 20-45 year olds who did not currently own saw the major barriers to achieving home ownership as the size of the deposit now needed in order to get a mortgage (mentioned by 57 per cent) and the high prices being demanded for houses (mentioned by 56 per cent). Not surprisingly, some found these problems too daunting to deal with: the proportion of non-owners who were saving to buy a home had been constant for three years, but in 2015 it fell by six percentage points to just 43 per cent.

As the Halifax concludes: 'Some people may be giving up on home ownership.'[11] But the main cause of this is not a change in their desires. It's a change in their belief that they can achieve them. If we want to explain the fall in home ownership, we will most likely find the principal answer, not in culture change, but in raw economics.

3

The bubble that
never burst

Rising house prices may dismay young people saving for a deposit, but for those who already own a house or flat, particularly if they live in London or one of the country's more prosperous regions,[1] rising prices represent significant capital growth, and hence an increase in their personal wealth.

How much money do owner-occupiers make from owning a house?

In 1986, in the research for *A Nation of Home Owners*, my colleagues and I carried out an in-depth survey of home owners and council tenants in three predominantly working class English towns. Burnley, in the depressed North West, and Derby, in the East Midlands, were relatively low house price areas (the average price of a semi-detached house in these towns in 1986 was around £25,000). The third was Slough, an industrial town to the west of London where average house prices were almost double those in the other two towns. But none of these towns was affluent or fashionable, and all had large working class and Asian-immigrant populations. They were chosen precisely because we wanted to look at how the spread of home ownership had changed the lives of 'ordinary' English households.

We interviewed 150 households in each town to gather precise details on their housing histories. We tracked every move they'd made since becoming an independent household, and for owner-occupiers we recorded every purchase and sale price, every deposit and every mortgage. Few people had any trouble remembering these details, which itself told us something about the significance they attached to their housing as an investment.

We then calculated how much money (if any) these people had accumulated as a result of owning (and buying and selling) houses. We found that their median annual gross capital gain in 1986 prices was £2,000. In other words, on average, for each year they had spent in home ownership, their housing wealth had risen by £2,000 over and above anything they had spent on home improvements or their initial deposit. Even if their cumulative spending on mortgage repayments were deducted,[2] their median net annual gain was still £1,273.

These may not sound like large sums of money, until we remember that average earnings in 1986 were only £7,551. People's annual gross capital gains from owning a house were therefore averaging 26 per cent of their earnings; even after taking account of mortgage costs, net annual gains were 17 per cent of average earnings. For most people, therefore, capital gains from the housing market far exceeded anything they could have saved out of their earnings.[3]

People who had moved several times ('trading up') tended to accumulate more than those who had stayed put. Those living in more expensive houses had generally made more than those in terraced houses at the bottom end of the market. Gains in Slough were, on average, higher than in Burnley and Derby. Booms and slumps in the housing market meant that gains also depended to some extent on when people first bought, and how long they had owned. But on average, these home owners in three very modest towns had accumulated a £22,750 gross gain (£13,527 net of mortgage costs) in the course of their housing careers – over £60,000 gross (£36,000 net) in today's prices.

I am unaware of any recent research that has replicated this study. But since house prices have risen much faster since 1986 than before, we can assume that if average annual capital gains were calculated today, they would be significantly greater than we recorded back then. Even if they were still 'only' 26 per cent of average earnings, this would mean that average owner-occupiers today would have accumulated around £6,600 for every year they have spent as home owners. For those in London and other high-price regions, the actual figure is almost certainly much higher.[4]

We saw in chapter 1 that these are not mere 'notional' gains. This is wealth that can be drawn down later in life, used as collateral to raise loans, or passed on to the next generation. But where does this money come from? If home owners have for decades been making serious capital gains from the rising value of their houses, who has been losing?

Have we been robbing our children?

It is often assumed that capital gains are made at the expense of the next generation of buyers. Existing owners are said to accumulate wealth by selling their houses at a mark-up to new buyers who must therefore pay more to get a foot on the housing ladder than their parents did.[5]

But if each generation has to pay more for its housing than the previous one did, fewer people in each new generation would be able to afford to buy a house. Gradually, the number of buyers would dwindle, house prices would start to fall, and all those capital gains would get wiped out. But (up until the turn of the century), this is not what has happened in Britain. Historically, the housing market has lurched between booms and slumps, but owners have for many years been making capital gains while new entrants have continued to enter the market in ever-increasing numbers.

We can track the post-war history of booms and slumps in Britain's housing market in the two graphs in Figure 3. Figure 3a plots house prices (HPI, the Nationwide House Price Index), average earnings (AEI, an Average Earnings Index) and the general rate of inflation (RPI, the Retail Price Index) since 1960. All three measures have been made comparable by indexing them with their 1960 values set at 1.

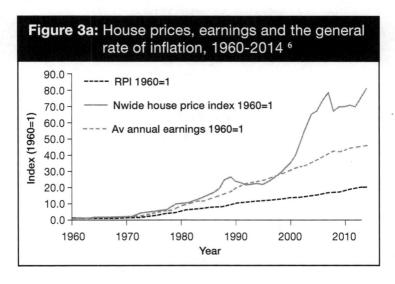

Figure 3a: House prices, earnings and the general rate of inflation, 1960-2014 [6]

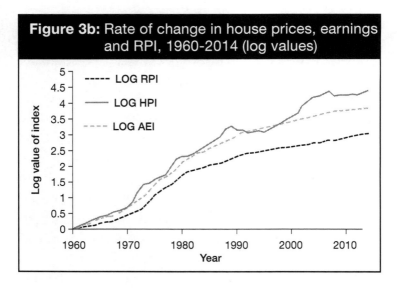

Figure 3b: Rate of change in house prices, earnings and RPI, 1960-2014 (log values)

Figure 3b contains the same data as Figure 3a, but this time expressed on a natural logarithmic scale to allow us directly to compare rates of change in different time periods. In Figure 3b, the same rate of growth will generate the same slope in the graph, whether it be, say, a doubling in an early year from five to 10, or a doubling in a later year from 50 to 100 (in Figure 3a the former will appear much flatter than the latter because it plots absolute rather than proportionate changes).[7]

We can clearly see from Figure 3b the four big house price booms (the four steep spikes in the *Log HPI* line) that have occurred in Britain since 1970:

- The first started in 1971. The Nationwide House Price Index (HPI), which began in 1952 with a value of 100, had risen slowly and steadily through the fifties and sixties to reach 242 in 1970. But then it suddenly jumped to 293 in 1971, 417 in 1972 and 517 in 1973 before slowing down again. In just four years, average house prices increased by 114 per cent (way ahead of the growth in average earnings of

43 per cent over the same period). As the slope of the *Log HPI* line shows in Figure 3b, this was the sharpest rate of house price growth we have ever experienced in Britain (before or since).

- The second boom started in the late seventies. The Nationwide HPI stood at 696 in 1977, but rose to 890 in 1978 and reached 1162 in 1979 – a rise in average house prices of 67 per cent in just three years. Again, this easily outstripped the average earnings growth over these three years of just 30 per cent.

- Next came the boom of the late eighties. By 1987, the HPI stood at 2346. The following year it reached 3028 – a 29 per cent increase in just one year. The index rose again in 1989, bringing the rise in house prices to 38 per cent in two years, before falling back below 3000 for the next seven years (the long period of recession and 'negative equity' for home owners that blighted John Major's premiership).

- Finally came the Brown boom of the early 2000s. Notwithstanding Chancellor Gordon Brown's proud and fateful boast to have 'abolished boom and bust', the Nationwide HPI rose steadily every year from 1997 (HPI=3270) to 2000 (HPI=4217) and then went into overdrive, reaching 9730 in 2007 before falling back after the 2008 global financial crisis hit. In the eight years between 2000 and 2007, house prices rose by 131 per cent while average earnings rose just 34 per cent. This fourth boom was the country's longest, and although the average rate of growth of prices in the early seventies was sharper, its sustained duration made it the biggest house price inflation ever. Indeed, given the resumption of house price inflation in many parts of the country since 2008, it might be argued that this fourth boom has never really ended.

Reviewing the history of these four house price booms, it would be easy to conclude that the huge wealth gains made by existing owner-occupiers must have come at the expense of new buyers entering the market, for in every case prices ran far ahead of people's earnings (mapped in Figure 3b by the *Log AEI* line). But a glance again at Figure 3b shows that, in the first three booms, house prices fairly quickly came back into line with earnings (indeed, after the 1990 boom, they fell back below earnings for a while), which suggests that in real terms (relative to earnings) buying a house became no more expensive for new buyers as a result of these three booms than it had been for earlier generations of purchasers. The capital gains enjoyed by existing owners cannot therefore have been achieved at their expense.

The first three housing booms: sharing the proceeds of economic growth

In the first three booms, even though house prices surged, earnings soon caught up, which means new entrants to the housing market ended up paying no more for their houses (relative to their income) than earlier generations had for theirs. Historically, the ratio of median house prices to median earnings fluctuated at or just above 3:1 across this whole period.[8] This means that although housing rose in price, it did not increase in cost (relative to earnings). Existing owners made capital gains, but their enhanced wealth did not come at the expense of new buyers.

So where did their capital gains come from? If we look again at Figure 3a, the answer is obvious. In the 40 years between 1960 and 1999, average house prices rose by 3,104 per cent (Nationwide HPI up from 123.2 to 3,947.5);

average earnings rose by 2,803 per cent (from £545.06 per annum to £15,825); but the general rate of inflation rose by 'only' 1,228 per cent (RPI, measured at a 1986 base of 100, up from 12.6 in 1960 to 167.3 in 1999). So while house prices and earnings rose more-or-less in tandem, other prices in the economy rose much more slowly.

The fact that earnings rose more than twice as fast as RPI is testimony to the long-term (if modest) growth of the British economy over these 40 years. Some of the rewards of this economic growth were enjoyed by the working population in the form of higher real earnings which more than doubled during this period. A worker in 1999 would only have needed to work for 24 minutes to earn enough to buy goods or services which a worker in 1960 would have had to have worked an hour to afford. The latter had become more than twice as well off as the former.

But workers did not take all the rewards of economic growth during this period. Shareholders benefited from higher dividends; welfare recipients benefited from higher pensions and allowances; and, as we can see from Figure 3a, home owners benefited from higher real house prices. Unlike most other commodities, the real price of houses held firm relative to wages between 1960 and the late nineties (earnings and house prices rose together, and both rose a lot faster than RPI). This meant new buyers continued to spend the same proportion of their earnings on house purchase as previous generations had done, thereby passing on to existing owner-occupiers a slice of the increased affluence they were enjoying in their wage packets. Owners therefore enjoyed real capital growth in their homes, but because houses were no more expensive relative to earnings than before, they were able to make these gains without new buyers losing.

Seen in this way, owning a house was, until the turn of the century, a bit like owning a share certificate in the British economy. The capital gains that home owners enjoyed were a 'dividend' financed by economic growth and paid out to all those who owned a little slice of the country.

The fourth boom: ripping off the kids

But now look again at Figure 3b, and this time focus on the period since the late nineties. The earnings and RPI lines are no longer diverging; average earnings over the last 15 years or so have only been tracking average prices. This means that in real terms, workers have been getting no better off. Between 2000 and 2014, average earnings rose by 51 per cent (from £16,545 to £25,029), but the RPI rose 49 per cent (from 172.2 to 257.4). Living standards have been flat-lining.

In this situation, we might have expected house prices to have flat-lined too, maintaining their long-term link to earnings. Instead, while earnings rose by only 51 per cent, average house prices rose by an astonishing 132 per cent. House prices have not only easily outstripped RPI, but they have easily outstripped earnings too. This means that since 2000, houses have been getting a lot more expensive for those seeking entry to owner-occupation. This has been true in most parts of the UK, but it has been especially marked in London.[9] The historic house price:income median multiple of around 3:1 has blown out to closer to 5:1 across much of the UK, and has reached 8.5:1 in Greater London.[10] Not surprisingly, London has the lowest home ownership rate in the country (more than 50 per cent of Londoners rent).[11]

Nor is there any sign that house prices may be falling back towards earnings, as happened relatively quickly in the previous three house price booms. Since 2008, it looks from Figure 3b that they have ceased to race further ahead of earnings, but there is no sign of them coming back into alignment. Indeed, in 2015 (Figure 3b stops at 2014) we learned that average house prices have started rising faster again – the Halifax reported an average 9.7 per cent rise in the year to October – and Savills estate agency forecast a 17 per cent rise by 2020.[12] A bubble which has been over-inflated for 15 years does not look like it's going to deflate any time soon.[13] As the Financial Times noted at the end of 2015: 'House prices are in perma-boom. Even the banking crash barely disturbed their upward march.'[14]

Since 2000, therefore, home owners have been making large capital gains, but most of this has been at the expense of new buyers, rather than a share in the proceeds of economic growth and rising general affluence. This is the first time this has happened, and it means we are in new, uncharted waters. Unlike the earlier three house price booms, this one really has made housing much more expensive for the younger generation to buy. If we want an explanation for the fall in home ownership rates, this appears to be it.

In his influential 2010 book, *The Pinch*, David Willetts complained that the baby boomer generation had 'stolen their children's future'. He pointed to the huge increase in government debt which future generations will have to finance; the massive, unfunded, state pension liabilities which they will have to shoulder; the student debts they have been required to take on; the additional provisions they will have to make for their own old age now that most defined-benefit pension schemes have disappeared outside the public sector; and the additional burdens placed on them by the growing health and care costs of an ageing population. But over and above all of this, he singled out the house price inflation since the turn of the century as the sharpest example of growing inter-generational inequity and injustice:

> Housing is fundamental to shifts in power and wealth between generations. The house price boom of the past fifteen years drove the biggest shift in wealth between the generations since the war... And where does this money that we thought we had come from? From our children.[15]

Willetts is right. In this fourth boom, unlike the previous three, home owners have accumulated wealth at the expense of the younger generation of prospective buyers – their children and grandchildren. This has in turn priced owner-occupied housing out of the reach of increasing numbers of younger households. According to the Council of Mortgage Lenders, 64 per cent of people born in 1960 and 1970 were buying their own home by the age of 35, but for those born in 1980, this figure has fallen to 44 per cent.[16]

As the owner-occupancy rate among younger people has fallen, so the numbers renting privately have escalated. With its flexibility (and lack of long-term tenure security), the private rented sector is most appropriate for young, single people, students and those in the early stages of their careers who need to be free to move around in search of the best jobs. But by 2015, the most common household type found renting privately was young families with children. Their numbers have trebled in just 10 years.

Six out of 10 private sector tenants say they expect to buy their own homes at some point in the future, but the median renter has accumulated just one-twentieth of the deposit they will need to make this transition. Two-thirds of them have savings of less than £1,500.[17] It is a bitter irony that Thatcher's children have grown up to become 'Generation Rent'.

Yet there is something about this generational home ownership crunch that still needs explaining. Given that houses have become so much more expensive over the last 15 years, how have getting on for half of younger households still been able to find the money to keep buying them?

Fools' Gold: How expensive houses have been made 'affordable' after the fourth boom

To answer this, we have to remember that the ratio of average earnings to average house prices is not the only

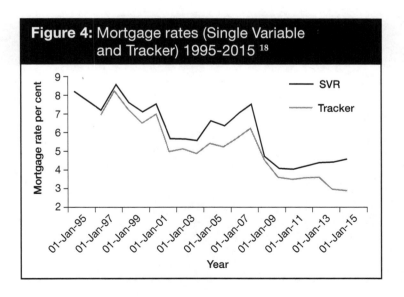

Figure 4: Mortgage rates (Single Variable and Tracker) 1995-2015 [18]

determinant of affordability. As well as the price you pay for a house, what also matters are the terms of the loan you take out to buy it. And in the last 15 years, as houses became increasingly expensive, so housing loans became much cheaper.

Figure 4 charts shifts in mortgage interest rates since the late nineties, when borrowers were paying around eight per cent on their housing loans. At that time, inflation was running at around two per cent, so the 'real' interest rate (stripping out the declining value of the loan due to inflation) was historically high at around five-to-six per cent.[19] But house prices were relatively 'low'. Prices had only just started recovering from the slump in the early nineties, and for a time in the middle of the decade, the rate of growth of house prices even fell below that of earnings. So although new buyers were having to pay high interest rates on their loans, the real price of houses was falling, which made house purchase increasingly affordable. This can be seen in Figure 5 which shows that the average mortgage costs

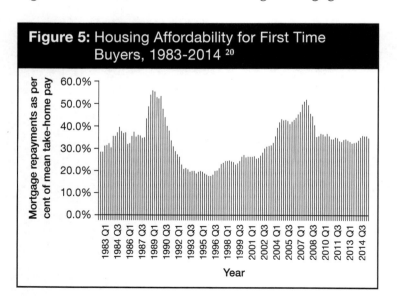

Figure 5: Housing Affordability for First Time Buyers, 1983-2014 [20]

of first-time buyers fell from more than 50 per cent of their take-home pay in 1990 to about 20 per cent in 1996.

From the late nineties onwards, however, house prices started to recover. Mortgage interest rates remained in the five-seven per cent range (slightly lower for 'Lifetime Tracker' mortgages[21]), but with house prices now racing ahead of earnings, it became increasingly difficult for potential new entrants to afford to buy. Figure 5 shows how affordability for new buyers deteriorated steadily, so that by 2008, mortgage costs were again soaking up half their take-home pay.

Housing costs at this level are unsustainable in the long term – few households can afford to give up half their take-home pay over a long period just to service the mortgage. So as the situation worsened, lenders came up with all sorts of bizarre strategies to try to keep squeezed first-time buyers in the market.

Old, cautiously conservative lending criteria were jettisoned as borrowers were offered no-deposit loans, 105 per cent or even 110 per cent mortgage advances, interest-only loans, loans based on inflated, self-certified incomes, and extended repayment periods. Anybody could see that the market had become stretched beyond breaking point.

At this point, we would have expected house prices to crash in real terms, just as they did after the late eighties boom when affordability became similarly tightly-stretched. Following that boom, house prices fell (in money as well as real terms) and the market stagnated for several years as earnings slowly caught up. Some 1.7 million households were trapped in 'negative equity' (they owed more on their homes than the property was worth), mortgage defaults escalated and house repossessions increased four-fold.[22] But in the end, the correction worked, housing became affordable again, and new buyers were once again able to enter the market.

But none of this happened in Britain in 2008 (even though it did happen in other countries which had experienced a similar house price explosion).[23] UK house prices did fall a bit (the Nationwide House Price Index dropped from 465 in 2007 to 396 in 2008 – a reduction of 15 per cent), but this only took house prices back to their 2005 level, and a year later they started inching back up again. This was nowhere near a big enough adjustment to bring prices back into line with average earnings, as had happened after all three previous housing booms. Even in 2005, average mortgage costs were absorbing a monstrous 42 per cent of the take-home pay of first-time buyers. House prices needed to drop much further than this.

The reason they didn't was that Britain was hit in 2008 by the global financial crisis (which itself had its origins in reckless lending to high-risk home buyers in the US, encouraged by the Clinton and Bush Senior administrations).[24] Fearing a major economic depression on the scale of the 1930s, the Bank of England slashed its base lending rate to an historically unprecedented 0.5 per cent, while the government bought the bad debts of failing banks to keep them afloat, and set about refinancing the banks and pumping up consumer demand by throwing billions of pounds of new money into the economy by means of 'Quantitative Easing'. The British economy was, as a result, kept afloat (just) – but we were floating on a sea of cheap money. Predictably, much of this cheap credit went straight into the property market.[25]

With the Bank of England base rate set at an historic low of 0.5 per cent, where it has remained (at the time of writing) for an unprecedented seven years, mortgages became much cheaper, and this made inflated house prices more 'affordable' for first-time buyers.[26] Housing loans at between two per cent and three per cent interest became common. This was not much higher than the general inflation rate, which meant many borrowers were effectively servicing their mortgages for nothing.[27] As we see in Figure 5, the average cost of a mortgage for those entering the market for the first time fell from around half of take-home pay to about one-third.

But this interest rate 'fix' left four crucial problems unresolved.

Chasing our tail: how we have made a bad problem worse

First, houses are still hugely over-valued relative to earnings. By enabling potential buyers to keep borrowing, low interest rates have kept this bubble inflated rather than pricking it.[28] Indeed, as time has gone on, the pressure has intensified, for as we noted earlier, house prices are again rising far ahead of earnings. The original problem has not, therefore, been resolved, but only postponed (arguably at the expense of the rest of the economy).[29] Dramatically-low interest rates have encouraged new buyers to take on increasingly huge loans to purchase housing assets that are by historical standards still over-valued by between 20 and 30 per cent.[30] Indeed, Ryan Bourne calculates that to get the average multiple of house prices to earnings back to where it was in the 1980s, house prices in the UK would need to fall by 41 per cent.[31]

Secondly, these loans are going to be very difficult to pay off in the future. Following previous booms, inflation has eaten away at big mortgage debts, rendering them manageable within a few years. But we are living in an age of very low inflation (the Bank of England repeatedly undershoots even its modest two per cent inflation target, and economists fret about the danger of deflation as a result of cheap Chinese imports and low oil prices). This means there is little prospect of the value of these huge housing loans being significantly eaten away in the short to medium term. To make matters worse, real earnings have hardly changed for the last 15 years either, so borrowers cannot look to future wage growth to help them clear their debts. These huge housing loans thus seem likely to remain a continuing burden for many years into the future.

Thirdly, repayments on these loans may be 'affordable' now, with record-low interest rates, but they will certainly not be affordable when and if interest rates return to a more 'normal' level (as at some point everyone assumes they must). Nobody knows when this will happen – the Bank of England keeps signalling that a rate rise might come soon, then putting it off – but the longer borrowing remains this cheap, the greater the shock will be to borrowers when the rise eventually comes.

If the Bank of England base rate were to rise to just three per cent by 2018, the number of borrowers faced with paying more than half their disposable income on their mortgage would rise from the current four per cent to somewhere between eight and 10 per cent (even higher than the six per cent level reached back in 2007).[32] In 2015, 26 per cent of borrowers could only afford to take out a mortgage by spreading the repayments over 35 years. Even in 2007, just before the crash, only 16 per cent of first-time buyers arranged mortgages over such a long period.[33] And as we shall see in chapter 5, even with these historically-low interest rates and extended repayment periods, many first-time buyers are having to be propped up with artificial aids like government mortgage guarantees and equity loans. As in 2008, borrowing is once again stretched to breaking point.

Finally, precisely because the Bank of England and the Financial Conduct Authority have become increasingly worried about the fall-out from any future interest rate rise, they have been putting pressure on banks and building societies to re-impose some of the old conduct and prudential rules governing lending. Lenders must hold substantially greater capital reserves to safeguard them against defaults. Interest-only mortgages are out, unless you can demonstrate a convincing strategy for paying off the loan at the end of the term. Self-certifying of incomes is no longer acceptable (which has made it much more difficult for the self-employed to get mortgages). One hundred per cent mortgages are a thing of the past. Loans are being limited to a smaller multiple of earnings.[34] And – as a consequence of this – new borrowers are now expected to put down a hefty deposit (often 20 per cent or more of the purchase price) before they are given a mortgage.

These rules are sensible (and were arguably long overdue). But the belated reintroduction of tight lending rules is delaying the entry of many first-time buyers into the market, and is shutting some out altogether. In 1988, the average deposit paid by first-time buyers was 10 per cent of the purchase price. By 2013, it had risen to 22 per cent (having peaked at 28 per cent in 2009).[35] Sums this large take years for most buyers to accumulate, and many never get there at all.

In earlier times, tight lending rules worked well, because house prices were within reach. But today, house prices are so high that saving for even a 10 per cent deposit becomes a daunting prospect, and 22 per cent looks hopelessly unattainable without outside assistance of some kind. In 2015, it was estimated that, limited to a mortgage of 4.5 times their income, workers earning £15,000 or less per annum (people like teaching and library assistants, dental nurses and care workers) would have to save for more than a hundred years to accumulate the deposit they would need to qualify for a mortgage to buy an average-price house![36]

So even if they can afford the mortgage repayments (at current artificially low interest rates) many hopeful first-time buyers cannot possibly save the tens of thousands of pounds needed for a deposit. We shall see in chapter 5 that some of the lucky ones are being helped out by their parents, who are cashing in some of their capital gains from the housing market to give their children a leg-up, and others are taking advantage of some ill-advised government schemes designed to subsidise first-time buyers' deposits. But many have no choice but to remain in the private rented sector, where escalating rents make saving for a huge deposit a soul-sapping experience akin to walking up a down-escalator.[37] This probably explains why fewer young people today are bothering any more to save for a home of their own.

Record low interest rates, therefore, may in theory have made house purchase more affordable, but many first-time buyers still cannot get a mortgage. As they have been retreating from the market, other buyers have been moving in to take their place. As we shall see in chapter 5, the demand for houses has remained high, but increasingly it has been coming from people who have no intention of living in them themselves.

4

Is tight supply the main problem?

We have seen that the decline of home ownership in Britain is mainly due to the dramatic increase in the price of housing since the late nineties.[1] Unlike the three earlier house price booms, the fourth boom, which began then and has never really finished, has permanently increased the price of housing relative to earnings, as well as in comparison with the price of other commodities. Ultra-low interest rates since 2008 have made these very high prices still appear 'affordable' for some first-time buyers, but a belated tightening of mortgage lending controls has jacked up the size of the deposit they are now required to come up with in order to get access to a mortgage. This has pushed owner-occupation further out of reach. Even if the high price doesn't knock younger households out of the market, the eye-wateringly high deposit probably will.

Can any of this be reversed? Can home ownership be made affordable for this generation, just as it was for their parents when they were young?

In a competitive market, if the price of a commodity rises, it is usually a sign that demand has increased, and/or supply has declined. If we want to understand the underlying causes of the great inflation of house prices in Britain since the late 1990s – the fourth boom – then we need to trace how patterns of demand and supply have been shifting. In this chapter we shall consider the supply side, turning to the demand side in chapter 5.

The peculiarities of housing supply

When it comes to supply, we have to recognise at the outset that the housing market is very different from the market for most other commodities. Four distinctive features are particularly important.

First, houses are fixed in space (when you buy a house, you cannot move it). This means that even if there are plenty of houses in the country as a whole, some of them may be in the 'wrong' places (places where few people want to live any more, or where there are no jobs for them to do). Even if the aggregate statistics suggest there are ample homes nationally for the number of households needing accommodation, there may be shortages in certain areas and surplus housing in others. Such imbalances can only be rectified by new housing developments in the areas that come under pressure.

Secondly, space is an inherently scarce resource (no two people can occupy the same space at the same time). When people start to find a particular place more desirable or advantageous than another – central London, for example, as compared with cities in the north-east of the country – the land area cannot be expanded to meet the rising demand, which means the price of houses there will rise. This problem can only be ameliorated if developers start to build at higher densities in the most popular areas, or if planners permit development on land that has hitherto been excluded from the market. In either case, the granting or withholding of planning permission by local authorities in the areas of high demand will be crucial in determining whether and how far supply expands.

Thirdly, about one-third of the price of a new house is determined, not by the cost of the labour and materials that go into producing it, but by the market value of the land it occupies.[2] Like any other industry, building can raise its efficiency and lower its costs over time, but the impact of productivity gains on house prices will be limited by what developers have to pay for the land they want to build on. Equally, if builders cannot get access to new land at a realistic price, they will not expand supply at all, even if the materials and labour are to hand. Any analysis of housing supply problems must therefore include landowners' willingness to sell as well as developers' willingness and capacity to build.

Fourthly, once built, houses generally last a long time. Thirty-eight per cent of the UK housing stock was built before 1944; 84 per cent was built before 1984.[3] Because each year we build more homes than we demolish, the total housing stock of the UK keeps growing even during slumps in the construction industry when new completions slow to a dribble. As Table 2 shows, the increase in the size of the housing stock over the last 50 years in Britain means that we now have considerably more housing per head of population than we used to. Between 1971 and 2011, the population of the UK grew by 13 per cent (from 55.9 million to 63.2 million), but the total dwelling stock expanded by 43 per cent (and the size of the owner-occupied housing sector rose by 86 per cent). As the table also shows, however, this expansion came to an end around the turn of the century. Since then, the total stock has been growing, but only in line with the rising population.

Year	TOTAL OWNER-OCCUPIED (m)	TOTAL STOCK (m)	TOTAL UNITS PER 1000 POPN
Table 2: UK housing stock, various years [4]			
1961	na	16.6	315
1971	9.6	9.3	345
1981	12.2	21.6	383
1991	15.5	23.6	411
2001	17.6	25.5	431
2011	17.9	27.6	441
2013	17.7	27.9	435

Because houses have a long life, many of the housing units that are traded each year are 'second-hand'. It is estimated that for every 10 homes sold in the UK, only one is newly-built, and this 10:1 proportion has remained pretty constant for the last 40 years.[5] This means that even if developers next year were somehow to double their output of new houses, the total number of homes on the market would only increase by 10 per cent, and the total housing stock would expand by less than an additional one per cent. Changes in the rate of new house building are therefore unlikely to have a significant, short-term impact on house prices.

We should also remember that new homes take a long time to plan and build (just getting hold of the land and organising planning permission can take years before the first brick gets laid), so any increase in new building starts will take time to have any effect in dampening down prices.[6]

Bearing all these points in mind, let us now consider whether and how far inadequate supply has been responsible for the spiralling price of housing over the last fifteen years or so.

The falling rate of house building

The belief that it has is widespread, and a glance at Figure 6 explains why. The graph charts the number of houses built in the UK for owner-occupation, council renting and housing associations between 1960 and 2014. It is immediately apparent that the overall rate of house building has been falling through most of this period.

Between 1953 and 1977 there were only three years when total housing completions fell below 300,000, but since then there has been no year when completions reached this level. Indeed, since 1990 there have been only four years (2004-07) when completions topped 200,000. We can also see clearly from the graph the impact of the 2008 global financial crisis. The total number of houses built in the UK plummeted from 226,000 in 2007 to 137,000 in 2010, and new supply has not come close to recovering since, creeping back up to just 145,000 in 2014.

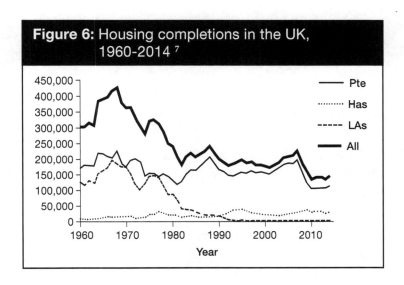

Figure 6: Housing completions in the UK, 1960-2014 [7]

In 2004, this long-term fall in the rate of new building led the Blair government to set up a review into housing supply problems (the 'Barker Review'). It found that UK house prices had been inflating faster than those in continental Europe for 30 years, and it put this down to the low rate of construction. To bring the long-term rate of inflation of UK house prices down to the European average (a fall from 2.4 per cent to 1.1 per cent per annum), the report calculated private house building would need to increase by 120,000 units every year (from 140,000 to 260,000).[8] It thought this could be achieved (among other things) by encouraging local planners to release more land for development.

Ten years after the Barker Review (and six years after the global financial crisis led to a dramatic fall in house building), the 2014 Lyons Report for the Labour Party suggested a minimum of 243,000 new homes would be needed each year, just to keep up with new household formation. It predicted a shortage of two million units by 2020 if current rates of output do not improve.[9] Lyons pinned the failure to build more houses on shortages of land being released for development (due in part to failures of local planning), a growing concentration of supply in a small number of big development companies (after many smaller builders collapsed following the 2008 financial crisis), and the sharp decline since the 1980s in public sector building.

Similar conclusions were drawn by another influential report, published in 2013 by the Town & Country Planning Association and authored by the late Alan Holmans. It also recommended that between 240,000 and 245,000 new homes should be built each year to meet the expected rise in demand from new households. Because new demand is growing fastest in the south, the report suggested that nearly a quarter of these new homes would be needed in London, and 60 per cent are required in the four southern regions of the UK. Two-thirds of new housing is needed in the 'market sector' (owner-occupation plus unsubsidised private rental) with the remainder in the social sector (council renting, housing association tenancies, private tenants in receipt of housing benefit subsidies, and council tenants who buy their homes at discount).[10]

The belief that falling rates of building have left us with a housing shortage which requires output to be raised to at least quarter of a million units each year to meet growing demand is now orthodox opinion among most housing economists in Britain:

- The (now defunct) National Planning and Housing Advice Unit argued in 2007 that England alone needed to build 270,000 houses per year (mainly in the south) to stabilise affordability;

- The Royal Institute of British Architects estimated in its 2012 Future Homes Commission Report that 300,000 new homes would need to be built annually to keep up with demand;

- When the Home Builders Federation updated the Barker report in 2014, it raised the estimate for the number of new homes needed each year from 260,000 to 300,000;[11]

- The Institute for Public Policy Research predicted in 2011 that housing supply would fall short of demand by three-quarters of a million homes in 2025 if current rates of construction were not dramatically improved;[12]

- In 2014 the Confederation of British Industry called for a doubling of new building to 240,000 per year;[13]

- A pressure group set up to represent the interests of current and future owner-occupiers, The Home Owners' Alliance, called in 2012 for 250,000 new homes to be built each year, concluding that building shortfalls are the 'fundamental cause' of high prices.[14]

Not all housing economists accept these conclusions, however. Neal Hudson at Savills Residential Research says it is 'simplistic' to assume that demand will keep rising due to increases in the number of households. Historically, he points out that new households only form in proportion to the availability of homes for people to move into, so if the supply of affordable housing slows down, rates of new household formation are likely to fall back (equally, if house building is stepped up, this will enable more new households to be created than would otherwise have been the case, and will probably attract more inward migration too).[15]

But while true, this argument ignores the question of suppressed or hidden demand. New households will not form if the houses are not available for them to live in, but this does not mean the need is not there.[16] Nevertheless, Hudson is clearly right to remind us that it is the availability of mortgage finance and the cost of credit which drive household formation, for they determine how many people can afford to buy the homes they need in order to establish new households.

It is also important to distinguish predictions about escalating levels of *future* demand from claims about *current* housing shortages. There is a tendency in this literature simply to assume that the fall in the rate of housing completions over the last 35 years must have led to a housing shortage, but it is possible that building eased off because demand was being met.

Projections of housing demand that suggest we will need a massive increase in the rate of building in future years may or may not be correct, but these future projections obviously cannot tell us whether construction rates in the past were inadequate. To prove that supply shortfalls were the principal cause of the explosion of house prices since the turn of the century, we have to look at patterns of supply and demand in the past, not the future.[17]

What limits new supply?

Those who argue that there has been a long-standing problem in building enough new homes in the past, and that this is what has led to high and unaffordable house prices, tend to explain the shortages as due to a combination of three main factors: the way house builders operate, the reluctance of landowners to release land for development, and the obstructiveness of planners who block new construction projects. Let us consider each in turn.

Is the construction industry too slow to respond to increased demand?

Some critics say there is something about the UK building industry that prevents it responding adequately to changes in demand for houses. They think the industry has become remarkably unresponsive to shifts in demand and that, unless prices are rising, it prefers to hoard land rather than develop it.[18]

Housing construction has a peculiarly long lead time, so we would expect a significant lag between the start of a house price boom and a change of gear from the building industry. But added to these long lead times is the notorious unpredictability and volatility of the housing market, which can change from boom to bust almost overnight. This creates dangerous risks for developers, for until their houses have been sold, they have a lot of capital tied up in both the land and the bricks and mortar.

A sudden downturn in the market, such as happened in 2008 (when the banks turned off credit and started calling in loans) can spell disaster for a developer caught with a stock of unsellable houses. In 2008 many small and medium-sized builders went to the wall, leaving supply in the hands of a relatively small number of larger companies, and they now seem reluctant to expand their output very significantly.[19] Even large firms cannot afford to get half way through an ambitious building programme only to find that the market has collapsed and they are left with hundreds of over-priced units they cannot sell.

Frustrated at the caution shown by developers in the face of rising demand, critics have sometimes accused the industry of sitting on land it already owns rather than developing it, waiting for prices to rise. Certainly it can take a long time for development sites to be completed, and developers are loath to continue building on land they own when prices look soft. In March 2013, planning permission had been granted for 6,500 schemes across the country involving a total of 400,000 new homes, but only 48 per cent of these were under construction.[20] Critics argue evidence like this shows that developers speculate in land – that they buy sites with planning permission and then sit on them as values rise, rather than building on them and selling them on into the market.[21]

It may, however, be more accurate to say that developers control the release of their land in order to avoid losses. All developers try to build up stocks of land so they can plan their output for several years ahead. They look to buy land when it is relatively cheap (i.e. when demand is low), rather than paying much higher prices to get hold of sites when the market is booming, and they then build on it according to their assessment of the strength of housing demand. A government review of the building industry in 2007 found that these 'land banks' are essential for stabilising firms' costs over time, and it noted that small builders are particularly vulnerable to downturns in the housing market precisely because they hold only small reserves of development land.[22] Similarly, when the Office for Fair Trading investigated complaints of land speculation, it found no evidence to support them, and it concluded that low rates of building are more often due to the inability of developers to get hold of development land in the first place.[23]

The fact that there is an average six-month time lag between a rise in the number of house sales and a rise in the number of housing starts suggests the industry tends to follow the market rather than leading it. This is supported by evidence that housing starts and completions in the private sector have for the last 35 years almost exactly matched the number of private house sales in the market as a whole. This suggests that when demand is strong, and house sales start rising, developers respond by applying for permission to build more new houses. When demand later ebbs away, and the total number of sales drops, developers respond by cutting back on plans for new building, they sit on the land, and fewer planning permissions get issued as a result.[24] House builders are, in short, price takers, not price makers.

The industry itself believes the problem of sticky supply has more to do with the activities of planners and landowners than it does with developers. The Home Builders Federation regularly surveys its members asking what they believe is hindering new construction. At the turn of the century, as the fourth boom got going, the survey flagged up two key drags on output: planning delays (cited by around 80 per cent of builders), and land availability/land prices (mentioned by about 75 per cent of them). Fifteen years later, these are still the two blockages builders are complaining most about.[25]

Is there a shortage of building land for sale?

Only 11 per cent of England's land surface is urbanised. If there is a shortage of development land, it is not because there are no remaining sites suitable for development – it is because these sites are not being made available to developers.[26] As we shall see, this may be the fault of the planners – but planners can only grant or deny the right to develop land when an application has been made to them. Before the planners have a say, landowners must want to sell their land for development. Developers cannot build unless landowners decide to sell.

Between 1983 and 2007, average house prices rose by 600 per cent, but development land prices rose far faster, by 1700 per cent. This suggests that landowners have been demanding much higher prices before agreeing to sell. At these prices, a developer has to pay an average of £45,000 to get a single plot large enough for one new home, and this price obviously then gets passed on to the final purchaser.[27]

When deciding what a plot of land is worth to them, developers look at what price existing houses in the local area are selling for and base their maximum offer on that.[28] But if landowners do not want to sell at this price, there is little (short of compulsory purchase) that developers, local planners or even central government can do to speed up the rate of new house building.[29] Even if planning restrictions were eased (and we shall see that the government has recently been attempting to loosen the grip of planning regulations), this would do nothing to change the incentives for landowners to sell any faster than they do currently.[30] According to Savills, the main bottleneck in new housing supply lies not in the planning system but in the release of land at a price which enables developers to build profitably.

Do we suffer from over-restrictive planning controls?
Even though only 11 per cent of the land area of England is developed, another 13 per cent is in the green belt, and 29 per cent is made up of Areas of Outstanding Natural Beauty, Sites of Special Scientific Interest and National Parks. Allowing for overlaps, this means that 40 per cent of the country is protected by law from development.[31]

In practice, development on the remaining 60 per cent is often prohibited too. Ever since 1947, when the Town & Country Planning Act nationalised the right to develop land, owners have had to seek permission from local planning authorities before building anything. Because new development tends to be unpopular with nearby residents worried about maintaining their property values and the character of their local area (so-called 'NIMBYism'),[32] local planning committees often come under intense political pressure to refuse applications. One quarter of all applications for new housing development in England are rejected.[33]

Many analysts believe these tight planning restrictions are the basic cause of sticky housing supply and high prices.[34] And there is research that seems to back this up.

One international study compared housing affordability across 378 metropolitan areas spread over nine different countries. It found that the places with the tightest planning restrictions are also those that suffer the most severe affordability problems.[35]

Within the UK, Christian Hilber and Wouter Vermeulen analysed variations in house prices over 35 years across 353 local authority planning districts. They estimated that house prices in the average local planning authority area in England would have been 35 per cent lower in 2008 had the post 1947 planning constraints on new supply never been introduced.[36] Even if planning controls had been applied less restrictively, they say house prices would today still be a lot lower than they are. If planners in south-east England (where development pressures are greatest) had been as accommodating as those in the north-east, for example, house prices in the south-east would today be 25 per cent lower due to the greater number of developments that would have been approved. Their findings, they say, 'point to the English planning system as an important causal factor behind the crisis'.[37]

Faced with evidence like this, political pressure has mounted for a relaxation of planning controls, particularly in the south-east, to allow more housing developments to take place in the hope that house prices might fall. Not just builders, but employers' organisations like the Confederation of British Industry have campaigned hard for looser planning restrictions, although these campaigns have often been fiercely resisted by local residents.

In an attempt to circumvent local opposition to more development, the Coalition government in 2012 announced a new 'National Planning Policy Framework' (NPPF) which established 'a presumption in favour of development' (although green belt land was exempted). Local authorities are now required to draw up development plans for their areas which anticipate local housing needs for the next five years and identify specific sites which can be developed to meet them. This is intended to give developers a predictable, rolling five-year supply of new building land. The Framework also stipulates that planning applications should be speedily granted where they comply with local plans, or where no local plan exists.[38]

Since the NPPF was introduced, net annual additional dwellings have increased by 25 per cent, although this has done little to dampen down the continuing rise in house prices. However, the CBI claimed in 2014 that only one in seven local authorities had been using their expanded planning powers to generate more housing.[39] Some local authorities still appear reluctant to grant planning permissions. In 2014-15, the 13 inner London boroughs gave permission for 11,970 new homes, but the 20 outer boroughs (generally more suburban and more Conservative) authorised only 8,000 between them. Kingston upon Thames, in the outer west, granted permission for only 75 new homes, compared with 3,000 in Tower Hamlets, in the inner east.[40]

The National Planning Policy Framework has now been bolstered in an attempt to release more land for housing. In 2015 the government proposed that local councils be allowed to authorise small-scale development of discounted 'Starter Homes' on green belt sites.[41] And in January 2016 the government announced it would supply developers with publicly-owned land where planning permission is already in place.[42]

Some analysts want to go a lot further. On the free market right, the Institute of Economic Affairs believes residents should be incentivised to accept more housing construction in their areas.[43] When planning permission for development is granted, land immediately becomes much more valuable, and the owners make a killing, but local residents in the area get nothing.[44] Local authorities may claw back some of the profit by negotiating so-called Section 106 agreements.[45] Developers commonly agree, for example, to include some 'affordable housing' in return for permission to build new private homes for sale. But this offers nothing to local residents who incur the costs of new development (in lost amenity, more traffic and overcrowding, and possibly a loss in local property values) but receive none of the gains.[46]

In 2011 the Coalition government tried to rectify this by introducing a 'New Homes Bonus' scheme under which central government matches council tax receipts from new housing developments for the first six years after completion.[47] But Kristian Niemietz wants to go much further. He suggests allowing local councils to keep more of the tax receipts generated by new developments in their areas so they can pass these on to local people in the form of lower taxes and/or improved services. He wants revenues from all housing-related taxes – stamp duty on house sales, inheritance tax on housing estates, capital gains tax on property sales – to go directly to local authorities, although he does not explain how councils in poorer areas would then manage to balance their books.[48]

He also urges that some way be found to compensate local residents directly for costs imposed on them by new development.[49] This would in theory defuse NIMBYism by setting up a clear trade-off for local residents between the costs and benefits of new development. But the practical difficulties of identifying losers and apportioning pay-outs appear daunting. And because compensation would probably have to be spread among many claimants, the amount paid to each person would arguably be too small to influence their support for new development.

While the political right puts its faith in strengthening financial incentives, the statist left seeks the solution in more taxes and government compulsion. The 2014 Lyons review for the Labour Party, for example, suggested that local authorities be given powers to levy council tax on sites where planning permission has been given but homes have not been built, and it advocated compulsory purchase of potential development sites 'where necessary'.[50] Similarly, the housing charity, Shelter, advocates 'more muscular approaches to land acquisition... through more widespread use of Compulsory Purchase Orders', suggesting that new, national development corporations could be empowered to buy land at existing use value, sell it on to developers at added development value, and use the profit to subsidise more house building.[51]

Are housing shortages the key cause of our high house prices?

What these diverse proposals from right and left have in common is the belief that high house prices are the result of an acute shortage of housing caused by landowners who refuse to release their land, developers who are sitting on their land banks, and planners who are cowed by local residents into refusing permission for new developments. But are these really the factors that have been driving up house prices? Is supply our key problem? There are five reasons for believing that it may not be.

1. Housing supply has expanded faster than the population has grown

Gordon Gemmill, emeritus professor of finance at Warwick University, says it is 'wrong' to talk of a 'crisis of housing supply' in Britain. He notes that every year from 1981 to 2008, the UK housing stock grew faster than the population, as a result of which the average household size fell from 2.65 persons to 2.29.[52] He concludes that the key factor driving the housing market is speculative demand fuelled by cheap credit, not inadequate supply.

Against this, analysts tell us that it is not enough for new building to keep pace with population growth. If housing demand and supply are to remain in balance, new construction must outstrip any increase in population.[53] Some existing stock is demolished each year which has to be replaced. Some locations experience faster population growth than others and therefore require higher-than-average rates of new construction (this is particularly true today of London). Some new houses are bought as second homes. And, most important of all, the number of households has been increasing faster than total population size. Largely because more people are living alone, average household size has been reducing, so we need more homes per head of population than we used to.

All this is true. But as Table 2 shows, up until the turn of the century, we *were* building at a faster rate than the population was growing! True, some of these new homes have been created by converting existing buildings rather than building new ones, with the result that the average size of units has been falling even as the number of units has been growing.[54] But this partly reflects the fact that household sizes have been getting smaller – we have more people demanding smaller homes. It is also true that for the last 15 years, the growth in total housing stock has only just been keeping pace with the expansion of population. But it remains the case that over the whole period from 1971 to 2011, we created enough new homes, not only to keep up with the growing population, but also to match the increasing number of households.[55] This means overall supply is no tighter now than it was 40 years ago, even allowing for smaller household sizes.

This makes it difficult to see how supply constraints could be the major explanation for the wild escalation in house prices we have seen in the last fifteen years or so (even though many commentators seem convinced that they are). There may be pockets of the country (notably London) where new building has failed to match increased population, but in the country as a whole there is still an overall housing surplus (in 2013 the Office for National Statistics estimated there were 27.5m dwellings but only 26.5m households).[56] The UK has a vastly bigger housing stock relative to population today than it had even in the relatively recent past, so how can our present problems of affordability be put down to tightening supply?

2. The timings do not fit

Secondly, the assumption that what I have called 'the fourth boom' – the big increase in house prices from the late 1990s, and the subsequent failure of prices to fall back into line with earnings – was caused by a past failure to build enough new homes does not fit the time lines.

The trend lines in Figure 6 show that the most dramatic fall in the rate of new building occurred between the late sixties and the early/mid eighties, 20 or 30 years before the fourth house price boom started. Conversely, total output of new housing stopped falling and started creeping upwards from the early nineties onwards, yet this was the period immediately preceding the onset of the fourth boom. Looking at these data it is difficult to see how falling supply can have been the proximate cause of our current affordability problem.

If supply is the key, why didn't the affordability problem arise 30 years earlier, when new building was plummeting? And why did the first three booms all come to an end, with house prices falling back into line with earnings, even though there was no significant improvement in supply? Indeed, the late eighties boom ended when new supply was still falling. Clearly problems of supply cannot have been the immediate cause of the spiralling prices which have overwhelmed us since the late nineties (although it could still be argued that a long-term shortfall in supply, dating back to the 1960s, created the conditions for the rising house prices we have seen in more recent times).

3. Countries which expanded supply still had high house price inflation

Thirdly, international comparisons reinforce the suspicion that supply constraints are unlikely to have been the key reason for Britain's house price spiral.

The UK boom from the late nineties onwards was far from unique. *The Economist* house price index shows average house prices in Britain, the USA, Australia and Canada all rising at similar rates before the 2008 crash.[57] And although price levels in the USA dipped more markedly after 2008, many other countries experienced a similar pattern of slump and recovery to ours. Indeed, the UK's real house price movements over the last five years look almost identical to the average for all OECD countries.[58]

Looking further back, over the last 40 or 50 years, it is also apparent that many advanced countries experienced a similar pattern of post-war house price inflation to that in Britain, with prices rising faster than the CPI but slower than average earnings. In the post-war period, Japan and Sweden experienced the strongest house price inflation, while Britain's trajectory over this period looks fairly unexceptional when compared with most other advanced economies.[59] This casts doubt on the claim that it was our long-term shortfall in supply of new housing, dating back to the 1960s, which caused the house price explosion around the turn of the century, for our price movements were not out of line with other countries over this period.

The key point about these international comparisons is that new housing supply across these various countries has varied widely. In some parts of the world – Ireland, Spain and US states like Florida and Nevada, for example – the turn of the century house price boom was accompanied by a huge increase in new construction, whereas in others – including the UK – the supply response was more muted. Yet what is striking is that, even where supply was dramatically stepped up, prices still surged.

The Republic of Ireland offers the sharpest example. Between 1996 and 2006, house prices there spiralled much higher than in Britain despite a feverish construction boom. A total of 700,000 new homes were built in Ireland in those 10 years – one for every six people in the country. Yet the average price of new houses still went up by 250 per cent between 1996 and 2006, and that of existing houses increased by 300 per cent.[60] The scale of this house price boom was vastly greater than in Britain, despite all that new building.

After 2008, when the bubble burst, house prices in Ireland fell by 50 per cent over the next four years, although they have recently been recovering. Thousands of newly-built homes were left empty and 20,000 homes on 'ghost estates' are now being demolished.[61] Clearly, Ireland's problem in the early years of this century was not limited supply; it was profligate lending by banks for real estate purchases which over-stretched demand. As we shall see, the same was true for Britain.

4. Construction of new homes for sale did not fall significantly before 2008

Fourthly, Figure 6 shows clearly that the fall in overall housing construction from the late sixties onwards was almost entirely concentrated in public sector building for rent. Every year in the sixties and seventies, local authorities built between 100,000 and 200,000 new homes for rent (although in many cases these were unpopular flats in brutal, high-rise or deck-access blocks, and they replaced existing houses which got cleared away as 'slums'). But after 1979, new council building dwindled, partly due to the ideological hostility of the Thatcher government, but also because the backlog of housing need following the war had largely been cleared by then, and population growth was modest.[62]

Councils' role as providers of rental accommodation for low income households has now largely been taken over by housing associations, but the rate of new building in the voluntary sector has come nowhere near to what councils on their own used to achieve. The result is that the total size of the UK social housing sector has fallen by 300,000 over the last 15 years.[63]

When we look at the number of houses built for sale to owner-occupiers, however, there was no significant fall between 1960 and 2008. Private house building in those years fluctuated a lot (between 100,000 and 200,000 completions per annum), but Figure 6 shows that the long-term trend over the whole of the period was more-or-less flat. It was only after the global financial crisis of 2008 that private house building dropped significantly from this trend line.[64]

Of course, the fall in construction of social rented housing would have had a knock-on effect on demand for housing built for sale, and this may have pushed prices higher. Some lower-income households which might previously have rented a home from their local council bought in the private market instead, and others will have rented from private landlords who in turn had bought in the private market. Even though private house building maintained a fairly constant level of output over this period, therefore, this may not have been enough to meet the additional demand created by the drop in building for social rental.

Between 1991 and 2003, private sector completions never fell below 179,000 (in 1992), but they never rose above 199,000 (in 1995). After falling from a peak of 242,000 in 1988, when the previous boom collapsed, new housing completions did not get back above 200,000 until 2004, when the fourth boom was already surging. So although building for the owner occupied market remained fairly constant, it is true that it did not expand to take up any slack that may have been created by the fall in building of social rental housing.

5. Increasing output in the future would have very little effect on house prices

The fifth and most compelling argument against the conventional view that housing supply is the main cause of affordability problems is that when supply increases, it seems to exert very little downward pressure on house prices.

One recent study monitored eight developments of around 300 new homes each built in the Midlands and the south by the housebuilder Barratt over a five-year period. All the schemes made a substantial impact on local housing supply, yet none of them affected local house price levels after they were completed.[65]

Now it could be argued that relatively small-scale local developments like these will have an impact on prices, but not necessarily in the immediate vicinity, and not necessarily straight away. However, economic modelling commissioned by the Department of Communities and Local Government suggests that for the country as a whole, increases in supply have a surprisingly muted effect on house price levels. Even if housing supply were to increase substantially in future years, the model finds it would have little impact on average house prices across the country.[66]

The model measures 'housing affordability' as the ratio of house prices at the 25th percentile to earnings at the 25th percentile. It then estimates changes in affordability between 2012 and 2031 if annual housing starts were to rise by 50 per cent, from 180,000 to 270,000 every year over that period (the sort of increase that many commentators have been calling for, and significantly in excess of the projected annual growth of new households). It finds that by 2031, the price/earnings ratio would have improved by just 1.3 points as compared with the base year ratio of 10.5. The home ownership rate would be just one-quarter of a percentage point higher than if the 50 per cent increase in new building had not taken place.

A supply-driven strategy for making home ownership more affordable would therefore have to dramatically increase output in excess of anything anybody is currently proposing in order to have any discernible effect. Such a massive building programme would have to relax planning controls, incentivise builders, force the release of huge swathes of development land (particularly in the south-east), and invest in extensive new infrastructure to support all this new development. And even then, the results would be modest, and would not be seen for many years. An increase in the rate of new building may be desirable, but clearly it cannot provide the answer to our current crisis of high house prices.

Conclusion: Inadequate supply is not the key cause of our high house prices

None of this means that attempts to increase housing supply are a waste of time. Most forecasts suggest we will need more houses in the future as population rises. And as Meen points out, higher rates of private sector building may only deliver small improvements in affordability, but these improvements are permanent and non-inflationary. 'Sustainable increases in homeownership,' he says, 'require increases in housing supply.'[67]

It is therefore worth investigating some of the proposals that have been put forward to stimulate more construction. In particular, we should look at how we might incentivise local populations to accept more housing development, and at relaxing some of the restraints on green belt development where land is of no great amenity value. But let us not kid ourselves. If we are going to resuscitate home ownership, it won't be enough simply to increase the number of homes we build.

5

New sources of demand

Although many politicians and commentators have focused attention on problems on the supply side (why aren't developers building more homes?), it is mainly changes on the demand side since the turn of the century which explain the post-Millennium housing bubble.

If we want to know how we ended up making home ownership so crushingly expensive for younger generations (and how we might begin to rectify this), we need to look at the factors that drove up and sustained the 'effective demand' (i.e. total spending power) for housing over the last 15 or 20 years. Foremost among these has been the flood of readily-available (and in recent years, extremely cheap) credit.

Easy/cheap credit for house purchase

Most house purchases are made with the help of a loan, and relatively few first-time home buyers have the money needed to purchase a house outright.[1] The 'effective demand' for owner-occupied housing therefore depends on how easy and attractive it is for prospective purchasers to get cheap or affordable mortgages.

Throughout the period of the 'fourth house price boom' – the big post-Millennium bubble – the Bank of England has managed the nation's monetary policy in accordance with inflation targets set by the government. This 'inflation targeting' began in 1992, after the UK crashed out of the European Exchange Rate Mechanism. Six years later the Blair government's Bank of England Act formalised it in law by giving the Bank independent control over interest rates and requiring it to maintain annual price inflation (measured by the Consumer Price Index, or CPI) at two per cent over the medium term.[2]

Figure 4 shows how this translated into mortgage rates. Typical mortgage interest rates fell from around eight per cent in the late nineties to between five and six per cent in the early years of this century, and then plummeted after 2008 to three per cent or less.

The five-six per cent interest rates levied before 2008 were enough to keep the general rate of inflation in check: the CPI varied in these years between 0.8 per cent (in 2000) and 2.3 per cent (in 2007).[3] It was this stability in the CPI that led Gordon Brown to boast that he had 'abolished boom and bust'.[4] But we now know that the low inflation at that time had more to do with cheap imports from China than restraint on the part of UK consumers. In these years, the British public went on a spending spree, maxing out their credit cards and scrambling after property, sending house prices spiralling. Unfortunately, the government's inflation measure totally ignored the price of housing.

Neither the Retail Price Index (RPI) nor the Consumer Price Index (CPI) includes the price of houses. The RPI does include housing costs (mortgage repayments, rents, council tax), but not the average price new buyers pay for their houses. The CPI does not even include housing costs. So the Bank of England's inflation target throughout this period completely disregarded the price of the single most expensive item most households ever buy – even when its price started spiralling upwards.[5]

As we saw in chapter 3, other prices may only have been rising gently in the early years of this century, but house prices were surging. Between the first quarter of 2000 and the last quarter of 2007, the CPI rose just 14 per cent.[6] In this same period, the Nationwide House Price Index rose 125 per cent.

Nobody at the Bank of England or the Treasury paid this house price inflation much attention, because it was not included in their inflation targeting measure. Treasury officials even decided in 2004 to redefine the growth of housing debt as 'increased savings', on the grounds that people borrowing to buy homes were building up their assets.[7] The growing bubble was redefined as a positive development! So as house prices surged upwards, interest rates remained where they were and government did nothing.

With house prices inflating fast, and the cost of borrowing held down at around five per cent, a speculative frenzy built up. Government monetary policy was functioning as an invitation to the population to borrow as much as they could to buy bricks and mortar. And as the boom got hotter with each year that passed, mortgage lenders became increasingly relaxed about giving people high loan-to-value mortgages which they could ill afford, for loans were secured against the expectation of further house price rises. The government and the financial regulators seemed happy for them to do it.

And then came the 2008 crisis and the fall-out that followed it. As we saw in chapter 3, belated pressure from the Bank of England and financial regulators has now tightened lending criteria, and this has made it more difficult for first-time buyers to save the large deposits they now need to access a mortgage. But against this, interest rates are now even lower than ever, so for those who can qualify for loans (including buy-to-let investors) the attraction of borrowing to buy more real estate is now even stronger than before.[8]

The problem is that the Bank of England is still targeting general inflation (the CPI), not real estate prices. Although it has issued various warnings about what is happening in the housing market (and in particular, about the continuing popularity of housing as a buy-to-let investment), monetary policy still does not target the specific inflationary pressures in that market.

Put simply, therefore, the first and main explanation for our current high level of house prices, and the decline in home ownership which they have triggered, is that government economic policy enabled it (and perhaps even encouraged it) to happen. The loose lending in the early years of the century has been reinforced by the ultra-low interest rates since 2008 to create an unprecedented 'double whammy' which has driven up house prices to unprecedented levels and kept them there. This has made home ownership for many young people both unaffordable and inaccessible.[9]

The growth of buy-to-let

Monetary policy was the prime mover, but other trends over the last ten to twenty years have reinforced the escalation of house prices. One of the most important has been the rise of the buy-to-let (BTL) landlord.

In chapter 1 we saw how working class owner-occupation grew during the twentieth century partly at the expense of private landlords. Saddled with tight rent controls and onerous security of tenure laws, many landlords disinvested from housing after World War II, selling out to their tenants at heavily discounted prices. As private renting fell, home ownership expanded.

Since the 1990s, the boot has been on the other foot. Private landlords have been returning to the housing market in large numbers, and this has increasingly been at the expense of new owner-occupiers.

The shift has its origins in the Thatcher years. First, the government abolished rent controls. Then it switched from subsidising the building of low rent council housing to subsidising the rents paid by low income tenants (housing benefit). Taken together, these two changes made it possible for both private and public sector landlords to charge market rents, even to tenants with low or no incomes.

The introduction of shorthold tenancies in 1988 then made private landlordism even more attractive by removing the right of sitting tenants to remain indefinitely in the property they rented. And in 1996 lending institutions introduced dedicated buy-to-let loans tailored to small investors, making it much easier to borrow to invest in the housing market.[10]

With all the elements in place, all that was then needed was a house price boom to attract people in. Many BTL landlords are more interested in capital gains than the flow of rental income, so when the housing market started booming around the turn of the century, new landlords were drawn in like bees to honey.[11]

Half of all BTL sales are for cash. Landlords who do need mortgages generally borrow on interest-only terms and use the rent to cover their monthly interest charges and their management costs. Much of the profit comes from the rising value of their asset. Hamptons International calculates that the average five-year return on £500,000 invested in a buy-to-let property has been a £100,000 capital gain (£250,000 in London) plus £92,024 rent (£118,468 in London). In London, the average landlord has more than doubled the value of his or her investment in less than 10 years, mainly as a result of escalating house prices.[12]

Once house prices started rising in the late nineties, BTL became increasingly popular (particularly among older people who had paid off their own mortgages). It offered strong returns and the investment looked very safe. And when the cost of borrowing money then plummeted after 2008, BTL investment became even more attractive, for loans became cheaper, rents kept rising and the returns offered on other forms of saving and investment shrank. As a result, BTL purchases kept growing and by 2015 they were dominating the market for new housing loans.

In the last 10 years, the total value of landlord mortgages has tripled from £65 billion to £200 billion. By 2015, BTL accounted for 15 per cent of all outstanding mortgages (up from just two per cent in 2000),[13] but for 80 per cent of all new mortgage lending.[14] It is estimated that there are now as many as two million private landlords in Britain, and they own getting on for one-fifth of the nation's housing stock.[15]

This remarkable revival in the fortunes of the private rented sector has often come at the expense of first-time buyers, for the two groups tend to be in competition for the same properties. Most landlords are small-scale – a 2010 survey found 95 per cent owned fewer than five properties.[16] And their purchases are concentrated at the lower end of the housing market, on the flats and terraced houses which have traditionally been the targets for first-time home owners.

In 2006, flats and terraced houses accounted for seven out of ten BTL purchases. The average price of properties bought by landlords was £156,000, well below the national average price for all properties that year of £201,000.[17] The property website, Rightmove, confirms that typical first-time buyer homes are also the ones popular with investors and suggests that competition between the two sets of buyers for one- and two-bedroom properties drove up asking prices by 10 per cent in 2015.[18]

When a prospective landlord is in competition with a prospective owner-occupier to purchase a house, the former enjoys a number of significant advantages. Even if the investor has to apply for a mortgage, her/his credit-worthiness is assessed on the rent the property is likely to generate, whereas the credit-worthiness of home buyers is assessed on their income. In areas of high housing demand (and hence high rents), this difference will often allow the landlord to borrow more than the prospective owner-occupier.[19] Indeed, landlords with several properties can leverage their loans to buy more, easily squeezing out buyers on low or average incomes looking to purchase their first house.

To make matters worse, the new affordability rules which have driven up the deposits demanded of first-time buyers and have stopped them applying for interest-only mortgages do not apply to buy-to-let borrowers. New affordability tests on BTL borrowers were introduced by the Bank of England in March 2016,[20] but prospective landlords can still borrow on interest-only terms (three-quarters of them do),[21] and they can still stretch the repayment period past retirement age, because the mortgage repayments are covered by the rent they receive. Again, this allows them to outbid prospective owner-occupiers who must budget to repay both capital and interest in their monthly repayments and to redeem the loan before they finish working.[22]

To add salt to the wound, while prospective owner-occupiers are trying to save for a deposit, they are more often than not living in rented accommodation, paying rents to the very landlords who have helped drive them out of the market in the first place, and thereby paying their landlord's mortgage costs!

It seems likely that the surge in BTL purchases since the turn of the century has been a significant reason why house prices have not fallen back into alignment with average earnings, as happened in the earlier housing booms. Since 2008 in particular, it seems BTL has been fuelling an already over-priced market.

Back in 2008, the (now defunct) National Housing and Planning Advice Unit estimated that only seven per cent of the increase in house prices between 1996 and 2007 had been due to the introduction of BTL lending. In 2007, the average house price was £183,000, and the Unit estimated that without any BTL lending, it would still have been £169,000. According to its model, prices were driven more by interest rates, income growth, mortgage availability and housing supply than by the introduction and growth of BTL.[23]

This contribution of just seven per cent to the rise in house prices seems quite modest, but there are good reasons for suspecting it is a substantial under-estimate. The authors of the report admit that their modelling failed to include houses bought by landlords for cash (because there were no estimates of their numbers). But more recent research by Bank of England economist Philippe Bracke finds that half of all BTL purchases are in cash.[24] This suggests that the impact of BTL on house prices could be double that claimed by the NHPAU.

It is also likely that the impact of BTL purchases on house prices has grown since 2007, when that study was done. Back then, BTL lending was worth £116 billion. Today it has grown to £200 billion (more than 20 times what it was worth at the turn of the century).[25] And this growth is still continuing, for the record-low interest rates which have been on offer since 2008 represent a huge incentive to BTL investors to buy more properties. Between 2008 and 2015, BTL lending increased by 40 per cent – 20 times faster than lending to owner-occupiers.[26] In 2015, house prices rose on average by eight per cent across the country. In that one year, lending to landlords went up by 40 per cent while lending to first-time buyers increased just five per cent.[27]

Figures like these suggest that BTL landlords have been pushing up prices significantly while at the same time squeezing first-time home buyers out of the market. This effect is exacerbated by the fact that they are often operating in the same (bottom end) sector of the housing market.

Belatedly, the government has recognised this. Since the 2015 Budget, the Chancellor has introduced four measures, all designed to reduce the attractiveness of BTL investment. First, he abolished tax relief on mortgage interest payments for landlords other than basic rate taxpayers. Next, he scrapped the 10 per cent automatic wear and tear allowance landlords have been able to claim against tax each year. Then he raised stamp duty on purchases of properties not bought as primary dwellings by three percentage points. And most recently, he lowered capital gains tax rates on assets other than residential property, which now carries an eight per cent surcharge.

All of this has been done in an explicit attempt to dissuade landlord investors from buying houses which might otherwise be purchased by owner-occupiers. 'People buying a home to let,' explained the Chancellor, 'should not be squeezing out families who can't afford a home to buy.'[28] The stamp duty premium alone means that a landlord buying a £275,000 property now has to pay £10,800 stamp duty compared with £3,750 paid by an owner-occupier.[29] This is forecast to exert a downward pressure on house prices as prospective landlords reconsider their investment strategies.[30]

But the government is also worried about going too far in disincentivising private landlords. Both the Bank of England and the Treasury are desperate to avoid a repeat of the early 1990s house price slump (even though a big reduction of house prices is arguably precisely what's needed to bring prices back into alignment with earnings). With loans to landlords accounting for 80 per cent of all new mortgages, the Bank has warned of the danger of a 'housing market shock' if BTL landlords were to start selling in large numbers. A stampede out of BTL, it fears, could crash the market.[31] Trading on these fears, the National Landlords Association warned in 2016 that the Chancellor's changes could trigger as many as half a million sales over the next 12 months as landlords scramble to disinvest.[32]

The government is trying to walk a narrow tightrope. It wants to deter investors from buying more properties (so owner-occupiers can get back into the market), but it does not want to panic existing landlords into selling up. This looks suspiciously like one of those 'contradictions of capitalism' which Marxists like to talk about. The Chancellor wants to stop landlords from pushing house prices beyond what owner-occupiers can afford; but he's scared of bringing prices down to a level where owner-occupiers might once again be able to buy.

There is a way out of this dilemma, but it does not involve taxing landlords into submission as the government is now doing. Rather, we could learn from the history of the 1950s when private rental and home ownership last came into competition with each other. Back then, home ownership was given a huge boost when tenants started buying their homes from their landlords. In chapter 7 we shall see how we might set about making history repeat itself.

Foreign billionaires investing in London

Another factor that has been fuelling the long-running fourth house price boom has been an influx of foreign money into the UK housing market.

Foreign direct investment into Britain has been booming – in 2014 it was running at £185 billion per annum (£72 billion more than UK direct investment abroad).[33] Some of this goes into building new firms or infrastructure that will create employment and raise living standards. But much of it involves purchase of existing UK assets, particularly property. The value of overseas investment in UK housing stood at about £32 billion in 2014 – up from £6 billion 10 years earlier.[34]

In 2015, Savills estate agency reported that Britain's housing market had become the fourth-most attractive destination in the world (behind the USA, the United Arab Emirates and Singapore) for foreign investors looking to put their money into residential property assets. Investors are attracted here because house prices have been rising, rental returns are strong, and the prospects for future growth are encouraging.[35]

Most foreign money goes into London, and particularly the so-called 'prime' residential areas of the capital such as Westminster and Kensington & Chelsea. Only 40 per cent of buyers in prime central London in 2013 were from the UK (and 60 per cent of the sales were for cash).[36] In the year ending June 2013, half of all £1m+ sales of residential property in prime central London went to non-UK nationals, with 28 per cent going to non-residents. The more expensive the property, the more likely it is to be bought by someone from overseas: seven out of 10 London houses sold for £5 million or more go to foreigners.[37] Buyers come mainly from Russia, Singapore, Hong Kong and the Middle East. Fewer than half of them use their UK property as their main residence. One in six buy as an investment and never live in it.[38]

This influx of foreign money may have generated some benefits for London, for much of it has gone into purchases of new 'off-the-plan' developments. Buoyant demand from overseas has reduced the risk faced by developers investing in large and expensive new building projects, and some of these developments may never have gone ahead at all without support from foreign buyers.[39]

The downside, however, is that all this overseas demand has also created another price stimulus and helps to explain why London house prices have soared ahead of the rest of the country. In previous booms,

London and the south-east have tended to lead the way, and other regions have caught up later. Not this time. Not only has the north-south divide widened and shown no sign of closing, but London has pulled away from the rest of the south-east too.[40] By 2015, prices in the prime central boroughs (Westminster and Kensington & Chelsea) were 63 per cent above their pre-crisis peak, compared with a London average of 45 per cent and an England & Wales average of just 7 per cent.[41] House prices per square foot in the capital are now the second highest in the world after Monaco.[42]

The Economist magazine denies that this influx of foreign money is responsible for Britain's sustained high house prices. It suggests that foreign ownership of houses is rare outside a tiny corner of the capital and it claims that in London as a whole, foreign purchases account for only about three per cent of the total.[43] Other estimates, however, put the figure for Greater London closer to 10 or even 15 per cent.[44]

As the Institute for Fiscal Studies notes, even if foreign investment is concentrated in the central areas, it creates ripples throughout the conurbation. Well-off British people who would previously have bought in prime London move a bit further out to where housing is (relatively) cheaper. This pushes prices up in these adjoining areas, in turn displacing aspiring buyers there who have to go to even more outlying neighbourhoods to find somewhere affordable. And so it goes on.[45] While the scale of foreign purchases is unlikely to have had much of an impact outside London, it could be a significant factor explaining why prices throughout the capital have pulled so far away from those in the rest of the country. For most Londoners, the city is now unaffordable.[46]

Family transfers

A fourth, new demand factor sustaining high house prices has been the increased importance of what journalists like to call 'the bank of Mum and Dad.' Younger buyers fortunate enough to have parents or grandparents who bought their homes have been getting into the market, either by using loans and gifts from their parents, or with the help of legacies inherited from parents or grandparents. In either case – gifts from living relatives or legacies from dead ones – most of this money comes from capital gains generated by an earlier and more fortunate generation of home owners. In this sense, the housing market is now feeding off itself.

Evidence on the scale and importance of housing bequests and gifts is hard to come by, but we do have some pointers. In 2015, six per cent of all first-time buyers bought houses outright for cash, while another five per cent took out mortgages for less than 20 per cent of the total purchase price. Most of these purchases were financed by family wealth: two-thirds of first-time cash buyers used money given to them by their parents, and one-fifth used inherited money.[47]

This still leaves nine out of 10 first-time buyers relying on mortgages. But even those who did not get their homes bought for them often relied on financial assistance from their families. One survey reports that more than half of first-time buyers received some help from their parents in finding the money for their deposit (not surprising when the average size of deposit was £53,000).[48] The Council of Mortgage Lenders confirms that in 2012, only 36 per cent of first-time buyers bought without any financial assistance from their families (before the 2008 crash, the comparable figure was 60 per cent). The increased reliance on family help in recent years reflects the higher deposits required of first-time buyers since the global financial crisis.[49]

Immigration and other demographic changes

We saw in chapter 4 that most projections of future housing demand foresee a substantial increase in the number of UK households requiring accommodation over the next 20 to 30 years. This is partly due to lifestyle changes (more of us will be living alone, for example) and partly due to increased immigration. Immigration in particular has been increasing rapidly since the turn of the century and represents the fifth key change since the late nineties to have fuelled the great house price bubble.

Between 2000 and 2014, 2.3 million new households were formed in the UK. Two-thirds of them (1.5 million) had a foreign born 'Household Reference Person' (what used to be called a 'head of household'). Recently, the rate of net immigration has risen even faster. From 2013 to 2015, net immigration increased from 209,000 to 318,000pa.[50] In the last five years, 90 per cent of all the new households that have formed have had foreign-born reference persons.[51]

Like BTL landlords, immigrants tend to compete for housing at the lower end of the market, where first-time buyers are also clustered. Indeed, most recently-arrived immigrants rent their homes from private landlords. Their increased numbers have therefore stoked up demand for cheaper housing, both directly (through their own purchases) and indirectly (through landlords purchasing houses to rent to them).

It is difficult to gauge the exact impact of increased immigration on house prices, but a 2008 House of Lords report suggested that if net migration over the next 20 years were reduced to zero (from its then projected 190,000 per annum), house prices would end up 13 per cent lower on average than they will otherwise be.

This looks increasingly like an under-estimate, for most forecasters nowadays expect immigration to far exceed the 190,000 pa on which the House of Lords calculations were based. The Department for Communities and Local Government estimates that what it calls a 'high' net immigration level of 217,000 per annum would generate demand for another 95,000 housing units every year in Britain until 2037. But net immigration to the UK is currently running at 330,000 per annum. Even if immigration settled at 300,000, this would mean an increase of 130,000 households every year.[52]

It seems clear that immigration has been another factor driving up and then sustaining high house prices. It also seems likely that this will continue into the future. One-third of household growth in England in the next 15-20 years is expected to come from immigration. Inevitably, this will fuel demand for housing, push up prices, and squeeze some people out of the market.

As we noted in chapter 4, there has also been a trend for households to get smaller. In 2013, three in 10 UK households consisted of one person living alone, up from two in 10 in 1981.[53] By 2033, the proportion is expected to grow to four in 10.[54] More people living alone translates into a higher aggregate demand for housing units, and thus another upward pressure on house prices.

This growth in the number of people living alone obviously reflects changes in patterns of family life, including the rise in divorce and separations. However, when families split up, they often recombine later in new permutations – about half of all break-ups result in new, merged households forming. Alan Holmans estimated that increased separation and divorce rates are contributing a net increase in the number of households of about fifty thousand per year between 2001 and 2021.[55]

The trend to smaller household sizes is not unique to the UK, however – it has happened in all north-western European countries with the exception of Ireland. Taken on its own, it cannot therefore explain the UK's specific housing affordability problem.[56] It is also a long-term trend which began long before the start of the fourth house price boom. Like the growth in the number of dual-earner households (another long-term change which has probably stoked up house prices by increasing household spending power), the increase in the number of single-person households is likely to have boosted housing demand over several decades. Although it is significant, it is not therefore one of the recent changes that might have created and sustained the specific surge in house prices since the late nineties.

6

How government policy is making matters worse

The main cause of the long, post-Millenium house price boom has been artificially inflated demand pumped up initially by reckless lending by banks, and then kept going by expansionary monetary policies adopted by successive governments.

First, between the late nineties and 2008, banks were allowed to lend on much higher multiples of borrowers' incomes than had been allowed in the past. Then, when prices had been driven way beyond normal levels as a result of people borrowing more than they could realistically afford to repay, the 2008 financial crisis led the government and the Bank of England to slash interest rates, so borrowing became cheaper than it had ever been before. Just at the point where the housing market needed a massive correction to bring prices back into line with earnings, this flood of cheap credit drove house prices higher still.

Today, as a result of these two huge boosts to housing demand, hundreds of thousands – perhaps millions – of households sit in vastly over-valued properties bought with massive mortgages which they can only just afford to service even at record-low interest rates. On some indicators, levels of mortgage debt, and buyers' vulnerability to any future interest rate rises, is worse now than it was back in 2008, when the financial system came close to a total meltdown. The total value of mortgage debt today is 15 per cent higher than it was then, and the average value of new mortgages is 22 per cent higher. Total household debt has dropped a bit since 2008 (from 168 per cent of gross disposable income to 142 per cent), but it is still as high as it was in 2003/04.[1]

Nobody knows what happens next; everyone is holding their breath. The market is stretched tighter than ever before, and for the first time in our modern history, home ownership rates are falling. Many young people have been shut out of the market because they cannot afford to buy, and even if they can, they can no longer scrape together the huge deposit they need to qualify for a loan. It is obvious that any significant increase in interest rates (to bring the cost of borrowing somewhere closer to its historical normal level) will trigger a tidal wave of negative equity, defaults and foreclosures that will make the misery of the market adjustment following the 1988 house price boom look mild in comparison. In the Treasury and the Bank of England, nobody dare countenance even a quarter point rise in base rate.

So in this dangerously precarious situation, what has the government been doing to salvage the future of home ownership? It has been stoking the inflationary fire with a range of initiatives designed to enable even more young people to borrow even more money to pay even higher prices for even more over-valued properties. Finding itself at the bottom of a very deep hole, the government is still furiously digging.

Help to Buy

The Conservative government's Help to Buy scheme is the core strategy for supporting and extending home ownership. Launched in 2013 at an estimated cost of £24 billion over the next seven years, the *Financial Times* described it as the biggest government boost to home ownership since Thatcher's Right To Buy in the 1980s. It offers mortgage guarantees, equity loans and a subsidised savings account, all designed to get people out of rented accommodation and into home ownership by enhancing their purchasing power.

These demand-side policies are electorally popular and do not threaten the property values of existing owner-occupiers. When asked what the government should do to make homes more affordable, home owners are six times more likely to support financial subsidies for first-time buyers than they are to accept increased development of new houses.[2] But this strategy threatens to inflate prices even further (house prices have risen 18 per cent since it was introduced) and to create an even bigger headache later on. As the Americans (and the rest of the world) learned when all those sub-prime mortgage debts went belly-up in 2008, engineering greater access to home ownership for people who cannot afford it does not represent a stable, long-term solution to the problem of affordability, and it can end up making things a lot worse.[3]

Although it dates only from 2013, Help to Buy consists of three main initiatives, two of which were already around in one form or another before then (indeed, one dates back to the days of the last Labour government). In 2013, these existing policies were brought together, re-badged and updated with some new additions added later on.[4]

Help to Buy equity loan scheme

The first plank in Help to Buy is a policy which helps buyers put a big enough deposit together to enable them to qualify for a mortgage on a newly-built property. In this way, it tries to tackle one of the main factors that has been shutting new buyers out of the market since the 2008 financial crash (although it has its origins earlier than that, in the Labour government's HomeBuy scheme). At the same time, it also aims to give a boost to the building industry by stimulating more demand for new homes.[5]

Under the scheme, the government provides an equity loan of up to 20 per cent of the value of the property being purchased, up to a maximum purchase price of £600,000. No interest is charged on the loan for the first five years, and the loan is repayable when the house is sold or the mortgage is redeemed.[6] The scheme is open to anyone wishing to buy a main residence. First-time buyers can apply, but so too can existing owners who want to move house, and there is no income cap.

The equity loans scheme was originally intended to run for three years, but has now been extended to 2021. The government predicted on launch that it would help 74,000 households with up to £3.5 billion worth of assistance, which implies an average equity loan worth £47,000. In the first 18 months of the scheme (April 2013 to September 2014), about four-fifths of the loans were to first-time buyers who purchased properties with an average value of £210,000. Given that the average value of all transactions in 2013 was £251,000, this indicates that the scheme has mainly been used by people buying cheaper properties.

Most purchases have also been concentrated in cheaper parts of the country.[7] However, in 2015 the government introduced an enhanced scheme aimed specifically at buyers in London who can now get loans covering 40 per cent of their purchase price.[8]

Help to Buy mortgage guarantee scheme

Launched in 2012 as the NewBuy guarantee, and later extended as part of the 2013 Help to Buy scheme, this policy allows mortgage lenders to offer bigger loans to buyers with small deposits covering as little as 5 per cent of the purchase price. People with deposits this small would not normally qualify for a mortgage under current rules, but under this scheme, their loans are guaranteed by the taxpayer, so lenders are more willing to take the risk.

As with the equity loan scheme, mortgage guarantees are limited to purchasers of homes worth up to £600,000. They are available to existing owners as well as first-time buyers, and there is no income limit on those applying. The scheme is due to run to the end of 2016.

In partnership with the lending institution, a developer agrees to put 3.5 per cent of the proceeds from the sale of the property into an indemnity fund. If all goes well, the builder gets this money back seven years later, but if the borrower defaults during that time, the lender not only repossesses the house and keeps the initial deposit, but also gets compensated up to the full value of its loss by drawing down on the indemnity fund. If there is not enough money in the indemnity fund, the lender can draw on up to £12 billion of government (i.e. taxpayer) guarantees. The government believes its ultimate guarantee is enough to insure up to £130 billion worth of mortgages (some 10 per cent of the nation's total housing debt).[9]

In the first 12 months of the scheme, most borrowers were first-time buyers and their median income of £42,683 was very close to the median income of all home buyers with mortgages in the country as a whole. The mean value of the properties they purchased was, however, only £156,000.[10]

Help to Buy ISA
Tax-free Individual Savings Accounts have been around for many years, but in 2015 the government introduced a special ISA for individuals saving for a deposit on a home. Valid on purchases up to £250,000 outside London and £450,000 in London, the Help to Buy ISA allows people saving for a deposit to shelter up to £12,000 in a tax-free savings account which will then attract a 25 per cent government top-up when they come to buy their first house. Effectively, this means savings in the scheme will earn a 10.6 per cent annual rate of interest, paid for by the taxpayer.[11]

Additional policies impacting on home ownership

The Help to Buy strategy is not the only government initiative designed to prop up effective demand in the housing market.

Starter Homes for first-time buyers
In its Autumn Statement in November 2015, the government announced 'the biggest affordable house building programme since the 1970s'. But unlike the seventies, when provision of 'affordable housing' meant building council houses and flats to rent to low-income tenants, this policy mainly involves private developers

building 'Starter Homes' for sale to first-time buyers. Buyers have to be under the age of 40 to qualify. They are able to buy at a 20 per cent discount from the market price, but they are prohibited from reselling or commercially letting their homes for five years.[12]

The 20 per cent price reduction is funded by relieving builders of their existing obligations to include other kinds of 'affordable housing' (e.g. houses to be managed and let by housing associations) in their developments.[13] Instead of extracting cheap rental housing as the price for granting planning permission under 'Section 106 agreements', this new policy requires builders to provide cheap houses for sale. The net impact on the supply of new housing overall will therefore be minimal; the policy will increase the number of houses for sale, but at the expense of those built for social rental.

Prices of these starter homes are capped at £450,000 in London and £250,000 elsewhere. But even at these prices (representing 15 times and 11 times average salaries respectively) it seems unlikely that many first time buyers will be able to afford them.[14] It has been calculated that to buy a £450,000 Starter Home in London, buyers need a £100,000 annual salary; even a £250,000 Starter Home outside the capital will be out of reach to anyone earning less than £55,000pa and will require a deposit of £47,000.[15] No wonder *The Economist* dismissed the policy as a 'middle class giveaway'.[16]

Shared ownership
The government has also been looking to expand existing shared ownership schemes (where people buy part of the equity with a mortgage but rent the rest of the house, with an option to buy it later).

Shared ownership schemes have been around in one form or another since the 1980s. The last Labour government legislated to enable selected groups ('key workers', social tenants and those deemed to be in housing need) to buy 25 per cent or more of the equity in their home and rent the remainder from a housing association, and in 2008, this policy was extended to all first-time buyers. In 2015, eligibility was further extended to encompass any buyer with an income below £80,000 (or £90,000 in London), and £4 billion of grants were made available to encourage the construction of 135,000 new shared ownership properties by 2020 as part of the 'affordable homes' building initiative.[17] Private builders, as well as councils and housing associations, are eligible to bid for these grants.[18]

By stretching the income cap to £80,000 or even £90,000 per annum, and by allowing existing owners as well as first-time buyers to take advantage of shared ownership, the government has implicitly recognised that even buyers earning three times the average income might not be earning enough to buy 100 per cent of their homes any more. This is almost certainly correct, for research on 145,000 households who bought shared ownership homes between 2001 and 2012 found that only 28,000 of them – less than one in five – ended up purchasing the whole of the equity.[19]

Rent to buy

In yet another initiative, the government in 2014 tried to find a way for aspiring home owners to save for a deposit without great chunks of their income disappearing in rent. This scheme (worth up to £400 million) pays housing associations to build up to 10,000 new homes over the next four years which will then be let at below market rents for up to seven years to tenants saving to buy a home. The impact and reach of this scheme is unlikely to be great.

Pensions into houses

Although not formally designed as part of the government's housing strategy, we should also at this point note the likely impact of a major initiative announced in the 2014 Budget which gave savers aged 55 and over the right to withdraw and use their defined contribution pensions in any way they want, rather than having to buy an annuity. The change came into effect in April 2015, when existing retirees were also given the right to sell annuities they had already purchased. Twenty-five per cent of the value of the pension can be cashed in tax-free, although the remainder is taxed at the retiree's marginal rate.

This change potentially affects about 320,000 people every year (the number who retire with a defined benefit pension). In addition, about six million existing retirees now have the right to sell their annuities. Six months after the reform came into force, the Financial Conduct Authority found that 200,000 people had withdrawn some or all of the cash from their pension pots. Sales of annuities plummeted from 90,000 in the second quarter of 2013 to 12,000 in the corresponding period in 2015.[20]

This reform releases yet another tranche of new money available for spending on housing. However, in many cases the sums involved seem quite small. Four out of five people with defined contribution pensions have £50,000 or less in their pots, and only four per cent have more than £125,000.[21] The Association of British

Insurers estimates the average amount being withdrawn is only around £15,000.[22]

Bank of England economists believe that only a relatively small number of retirees will have enough money in their pensions to buy property. They estimate that about 50,000 people per year plan to use their pension savings to buy property (mainly buy-to-let), and that another 15,000 per year will sell the annuities they already have in order to do the same thing. They accept that an additional 65,000 people wanting to buy houses every year 'could have an impact on house prices' (65,000 is equivalent to five per cent of all the houses sold each year), but they point out that those with smaller pots would have to top up by borrowing and that few would be able to get buy-to-let mortgages without other income. They conclude: 'it seems unlikely there will be a huge increase in buy-to-let lending on account of the reforms'.[23]

But even if they are right, and the pension reform 'only' boosts demand for homes by an additional five per cent per annum, this could cause big ripples in the housing market. At a time when the government is trying to rein in new BTL spending, it seems odd to have released a further 65,000 potential BTL landlords onto the market.

Paragon Group, a specialist mortgage firm, has reported a 102 per cent increase in the volume of buy-to-let lending in the year to September 2015 – up from £657 million to £1.33 billion. This seems to be the result of the over-55s cashing in their pensions to buy residential property as an investment.[24] The full impact of the pension changes remains to be seen, but when the government is trying to cool down the housing market and improve access to owner-occupation by first-time buyers, introducing a reform like this which will certainly increase the number of people with money to invest in buy-to-let seems self-defeating.

Illiterate economics (but masterful politics)?

Much the same could be said for most of the other policy initiatives we have been reviewing in this chapter. Far from making houses more affordable, the government's Help to Buy policies are almost certainly pushing prices even higher.

Former economic adviser at the Cabinet Office, Simon French, has taken issue with the *Help to Buy ISA*. Describing this as 'this government's worst display of economic illiteracy' (while conceding it represents 'masterful politics'),[25] French says this savings top-up can only push house prices higher by pumping another £835 million worth of demand into the housing market by 2020. He describes this as 'the next stage of a dangerous Ponzi scheme'.

Critics have been no less scathing about the other elements in the Help to Buy package.

Discussing the *mortgage guarantee scheme* for first-time buyers in London, *The Economist* magazine concludes that rather than raising home ownership rates, it simply gives a further boost to house prices. By enabling people to borrow more than they would otherwise be able to do, the policy allows buyers to bid even more money for the home they want to buy, and the result is higher prices all round. *The Economist* describes this as the government's 'pottiest policy yet'.[26]

The Office for Budget Responsibility seems to agree. Giving evidence to the House of Commons Public Accounts Committee in 2013, the government's independent economic advisers were in no doubt that mortgage guarantees drive up prices in the short term, and were extremely sceptical about claims that guarantees might significantly increase supply (and therefore moderate price rises) longer term. Historical evidence, they suggested, indicates that prices will rise and supply will hardly shift.[27]

The Institute for Fiscal Studies is of the same opinion. It calculates that if the mortgage guarantee scheme were fully implemented up to its maximum limit, covering 10 per cent of all mortgage loans, and assuming that none of these mortgages would have been offered by lenders in the absence of the guarantee (a strong assumption), then the scheme could be expected to increase average house prices by 10 per cent in three years.[28]

The *equity loans scheme* has also been criticised on much the same grounds. Boosted by an additional 20 per cent of equity, buyers can pay more than they would otherwise be able to afford for their homes. This may well have given the building industry a boost,[29] but critics say it is bound to have jacked prices up.

Interrogated by the House of Commons Public Accounts Committee in 2014, the permanent secretary at the Department of Communities and Local Government denied this. He pointed to evidence showing that most equity loans have been granted outside the housing hot spots in London and the south-east (56 per cent have been in the Midlands or the North) in regions where prices have been rising much more slowly. He thought this proved that equity loans have not fed through into higher prices.[30] The official evaluation of the policy published by the Dept of Communities and Local Government in February 2016 subsequently used the same argument to draw the same conclusion.[31]

But this argument is not convincing. There are many different causes of house price rises – nobody is arguing that Help to Buy is the only cause. Just because London prices have risen fastest, and buyers in central London have made little use of equity loans, does not demonstrate that these loans have not inflated house prices in places where they have been taken up. Even the official evaluation acknowledges that the policy 'stabilised' prices in these lower-price regions, which presumably means that prices ended up higher than they would have been without equity loans.[32]

Moreover, there is evidence that the average price of all homes bought using the government's equity loan scheme rose significantly more than the average price of all other newly-built properties after the scheme was introduced. A table in the official evaluation reveals that between 2013 and 2015, the average purchase price of all new dwellings built in England rose from £250,000 to £294,000 (a 17.6 per cent rise), while the average purchase price of dwellings bought with the aid of an equity loan rose from £186,093 to £231,224 (an increase of 24.3 per cent).[33] Even though most properties purchased with a government equity loan were in parts of the country where house prices were going up by less than the national average, the prices paid for these homes rose about 25 per cent more than the price of other newly-built homes bought without equity loans. This would seem to indicate that the government subsidy pushed prices higher than they would otherwise have gone, although it does not prove this was the case.[34]

Chasing our own tail

Critics of the various Help to Buy subsidies point out that, by pushing house prices higher, the government has been subsidising a small number of lucky buyers while making things even more difficult for everyone else. The policies, in other words, are unfair as well as counter-productive. As a recent Shelter report puts it, the policy 'has helped a small number of people to buy, at the expense of worsening the overall affordability crisis for everyone else'.[35]

In an admittedly rather crude analysis, Shelter estimates that the two main Help to Buy policies (the mortgage guarantee and loan equity schemes) have between them already driven average house prices up by £8,250. The charity suggests that total mortgage lending has been 8.4 per cent higher than it would have been had these policies never been introduced, and that this has pushed average house prices up by 3 per cent.[36]

In mitigation, we might note that Help to Buy is time-limited so should not end up making prices go ever higher. But history teaches us that once introduced, subsidy schemes like these are notoriously difficult to withdraw, for they create a new, higher equilibrium point. Already the equity loans have been extended from 2018 to 2021. If the critics are right that these policies have been driving prices higher, pressure will presumably increase on the government to come up with further subsidies, or to extend existing subsidies to more affluent buyers who find themselves locked out of the market. This is how we end up chasing our tail, with the government handing out ever greater sums of taxpayer money as house prices are driven ever higher by its existing subsidies.[37]

Economists tell us that in extreme circumstances, and for a short period, demand-side subsidies like these can be justified to kick-start a market that has stalled. But the housing market hadn't stalled when Help to Buy was introduced – prices were still rising well ahead of general inflation, and building was recovering after the 2008 trauma. Given that it was US government backing for subsidised, 'sub-prime' mortgages in America that got the world into such a mess in 2008, it seems the height of folly for the UK government to be relying on much the same sort of strategy now.[38] As *The Spectator* notes, 'It is as if nothing has been learned from that crash.'[39]

Indeed, it seems the government did not even bother to consider possible downsides to its Help to Buy strategy before ploughing ahead with it. The Treasury recommends that government departments should carry out a full impact assessment (including assessing alternative options) before proceeding with expenditures like these, but Simon French notes that no impact assessment was requested before introducing the Help to Buy ISA.[40] Nor did ministers call for an impact assessment before introducing the Help to Buy loan guarantee scheme, for in June 2014, the House of Commons Public Accounts Committee criticised ministers for pressing ahead with loan guarantees without an assessment.[41]

It seems the government did not want to be told whether its flagship Help to Buy policies were likely to work, nor even whether they might end up making matters worse. The suspicion is that ministers knew the strategy might pump up prices in the short-term while delivering few improvements in supply longer term, but they did it anyway, because they wanted to be seen to be 'doing something' to help home buyers. In time-honoured fashion, they stuffed more taxpayers' money into voters' pockets, just two years out from a general election.

7

Some modest proposals

'What is to be done? If a solution were politically easy, it would already have happened. It is not.'

– Martin Wolf, chief economics commentator at the *Financial Times*[1]

Some commentators seem resigned to Britain becoming a low-ownership society. The Building and Social Housing Foundation believes that the private rented sector will continue to displace owner-occupation and argues that private rental should therefore be made more attractive so more people will be content to live in it.[2] On the political left, where private home ownership has long been distrusted, influential politicians have welcomed the decline in the owner-occupancy rate. It's not such a bad thing, they say. We must rid ourselves of this obsession with owning our homes.[3] More disturbingly, some voices on the political right have started to agree with them, arguing that it is inappropriate for governments to try to support home ownership.[4]

Such reactions are defeatist and complacent. We shouldn't and needn't settle for this decline in owner-occupation. Home ownership is what the great majority of people still aspire to, and by spreading the distribution of wealth and strengthening people's sense of civic attachment and social belonging, it contributes vitally and positively to the quality of our national life. It is right that governments should seek to support and extend it.

But there is a clear need to rectify the gross generational unfairness which has arisen from the way opportunities for owning a home have shifted over the last twenty years. The Chancellor of the Exchequer, George Osborne, recently said in a speech: 'I don't want to give up on the aspiration of home ownership.'[5] This is a welcome statement of intent. But if he really means it, some difficult choices are going to have to be made.

Rectifying the generational inequity

Since the turn of this century, older generations have been enjoying record capital gains as house prices have rocketed. We saw in chapter 3 that, for the first time in our history, these gains have been made at the expense of the next generation of buyers, many of whom have as a consequence been shut out of home ownership altogether.

The collapse of owner-occupation among the young represents a generational process of social exclusion that is deeply worrying and extremely unfair. Fifteen years ago, 60 per cent of 25-34 year olds were buying their own homes; today, it is 40 per cent.[6] Every year between 1993 and 2003, upwards of half a million new first-time buyers moved into home ownership; by 2014, this figure had dwindled to 311,500 – and many of them were subsidised by their families or the taxpayer.[7]

As we saw in chapter 2, the sharp decline in owner-occupation among the young is not due to any sudden decrease in the popularity of home ownership in this age group. It has happened because home ownership has become too expensive for many young people to fulfil their aspirations. Those who have managed to buy are paying a lot more for the privilege: mortgage debt among home owners born in 1980 is 50 per cent higher in real terms than it was for those born 20 years earlier when they were the same age.[8]

This is a problem that has mainly affected the cohort of Britons born around or since 1980. We used to call them 'Thatcher's children'; now they are known as 'Generation Rent'. Some of this cohort may still be able buy when they get older, after they have saved a big enough deposit, or when they inherit their parents' house. But in the absence of new policies, many of them will never own. It is estimated that only 26 per cent of people under 40 will be living in their own homes by 2025 – a reduction from 38 per cent in 2013. Six in 10 of them will still be renting.[9]

Unless something is done now to help today's under-forties, the declining home ownership rate will be cemented into British society for decades to come. As older people (most of whom own their homes) die off, they will be replaced by a generation whose ownership rate is much lower, and as this cohort moves through the system, the overall owner-occupancy figures will keep dropping.

Even if we were now to find some way of enabling more young people to get their feet on the first rung of the home ownership ladder, the cohort in front of them – those born around 1980 – would still constitute a 'missing generation', for their prospects have already been blighted as a result of the events of the last fifteen years. Having missed out on home ownership when they were young, many in so-called 'Generation Rent' seem destined to remain excluded for the remainder of their lives. Rectifying this generational injustice by opening up a belated route into affordable home ownership for those who missed out earlier in their lives should be a major objective for any new policy.

Ways of making houses cheaper

We saw in chapter 6 that the government's principal strategy for reversing the decline of home ownership among the young involves subsidising first-time buyers so they are better able to meet the costs of high-priced housing. But this has had the effect of pushing house prices even higher than they would otherwise have been.

The alternative proposed by many critics and commentators is to boost housing construction by loosening planning controls or releasing more development land onto the market. But we saw in chapter 4 that even doubling housing output would have only a tiny effect on housing affordability over the next 15 or 20 years. When it comes to rescuing home ownership, proposals aimed at boosting the supply side are only likely to have a marginal impact in the short to medium term.

What is needed if we are to halt the slide in owner-occupation, and perhaps even start reversing it, are policies that reduce the price of housing to a level that people can once again realistically afford. Politicians may not want to admit it (given the desire of many existing owners to see their house price continue to rise), but the only sustainable answer to the crisis of affordability of owner-occupation is to make house prices cheaper.[10]

In chapter 5 we briefly discussed some ways this might be achieved. *Tightening restrictions on new immigration* would certainly help, given that 40 per cent of projected household growth over the next 15 years or so is due to immigration. Many new immigrants rent their homes, but increased numbers still push up prices by encouraging landlords to buy more homes to let. If the aim is to dampen down demand in the housing market, immigration is therefore an obvious (and politically popular) target.

Whether such a dramatic restriction would make sense for the wider economy is, however, a different question. Many employers are concerned to maintain high levels of immigration, particularly among skilled workers, and many immigrants probably contribute more to the nation's prosperity than they cost by driving up house prices. Besides, in the absence of fundamental changes in the UK's relationship with the EU, it would be beyond the capacity of any British government to deliver a significant reduction in migration from Eastern Europe or the Mediterranean, which is where most newcomers are arriving from.

Limiting house purchase to UK citizens could also help take some steam out of the market, though its effectiveness outside central London would probably be slight.[11] Seven out of 10 newly-built properties in the prime areas of London – boroughs like Kensington and Chelsea, and Westminster – are bought by overseas investors. The London property market has become a magnet for global investors looking for somewhere safe to park their capital, and this has helped push prices beyond the reach of all but the richest local inhabitants. Prohibiting purchases by non-nationals, as Australia, Denmark and Switzerland do, would stop this, although it might threaten the attractiveness to overseas investors of the City of London as one of the world's foremost financial centres.[12]

Reducing stamp duty would probably help bring more homes onto the market. Ninety per cent of transactions are for second-hand houses, so the shrinkage of the second-hand market has had a major impact on the number of homes available for sale to first-time buyers. In the late eighties, more than two million homes were bought and sold each year, twice as many as today.[13] We also saw in chapter 4 that the increasing reluctance of owners to sell has reduced the incentive for developers to build more new homes (for they base their building plans on the strength of overall demand).[14]

One factor in this increasing reluctance to move is likely to have been the escalation in stamp duty. A high transactions tax is guaranteed to put grit in the cogs of any market, and the housing market is no exception. Until 1997, the rate of stamp duty payable on residential sales was a flat one per cent (zero below £60,000), but in 1997 the new Labour government introduced two new higher-rate bands, and ever since then this tax has repeatedly been hiked by governments of all persuasions.[15] A buyer of an average-priced home in London today has to pay around £15,000 in what is now called Stamp Duty Land Tax. It is estimated that abolishing this tax could boost transactions by between eight and 20 per cent.[16] This would increase the number of properties available for first-time buyers to bid for (as owners once again start trading up) and should stimulate new construction.

Recent attempts by the government to *make buy-to-let purchases less attractive* could also help to take some excess demand out of the housing market. As we saw in chapter 5, mortgage lending to landlords has increased 20-fold since the turn of the century and is now worth £190 billion. One estimate from 2007 suggested that the surge in buy-to-let purchases only accounted for seven percentage points of the house price rise since 1996, but this almost certainly under-represents the full impact on prices today. Moves by the government to limit tax relief on mortgage interest for buy-to-let borrowers, scrap the automatic 10 per cent wear and tear tax allowance, and raise stamp duty on purchases of second homes by three per cent, have all been designed to reduce the attractiveness of housing to small investors with the aim of deflating overall demand. However, neither the government nor the Bank of England want to encourage large-scale disinvestment for fear that this could crash the market.

The huge growth in demand from BTL investors has been an important factor contributing to the house price bubble which inflated 15 years ago (and which still shows no sign of reducing). But rather than penalising small landlords by increasing the amount of tax they have to pay, a more positive, more effective and arguably more authentically *Conservative* strategy for tackling this problem would be to give private tenants a right to purchase their homes. We saw in chapter 1 that a major factor leading to the expansion of owner occupation in the 1950s was the widespread sale of privately-rented housing to sitting tenants. More than half a century later, it is perhaps time for history to repeat itself.

Extend the Right to Buy to all tenants

The Council of Mortgage Lenders suggests that one reason home ownership rates have been falling is that Right to Buy (RTB) sales of council houses have tailed off.[17] The last Labour government tightened the eligibility rules and clamped down on the value of discounts, and leftist administrations in Scotland and Wales have curtailed sales outside England. As a result, total sales have dwindled, falling as low as 3,000 pa by 2009/10.[18]

The Coalition government elected in 2010 increased discounts to try to reverse this trend, and the Conservative government that followed it has now extended the RTB to tenants in housing association properties who will also now be offered discounts if they buy their homes. This is expected to generate about 50,000 sales of social rented properties each year in the short term.[19]

Before he won the leadership of the Labour Party, Jeremy Corbyn proposed that the Right to Buy should also be extended to tenants of private sector landlords. He proposed that private tenants should be offered subsidised mortgage rates on their purchases, and that the cost of this should be covered by withdrawing tax allowances to buy-to-let landlords.[20] This is not, however, an idea that has commended itself to the Cameron government.

Corbyn's proposal was clearly motivated by the left's traditional loathing of private landlordism, and his idea for subsidising buyers' mortgage payments is in any case no longer viable since the Cameron government clawed back the tax allowances for landlords which Corbyn wanted to use to fund the measure. Nevertheless, extending the RTB to private tenants does not have to be motivated by class hatred, and Corbyn's proposal was not the only way of achieving it.

We have, of course, to be mindful of the rights of property owners to enjoy the benefits of their investment. But against this has to be balanced the disadvantages currently being suffered by a generation which has been shut out of ownership partly as a result of the surge in landlord purchasing. Landlords who bought properties early in the boom years have enjoyed windfall profits far in excess of any normal rate of return they might have expected on their capital, and these gains have been achieved at minimal risk. Meanwhile, many in the generation behind them cannot afford to buy their homes. The policy challenge is to extend a Right to Buy to tenants in the private sector who wish to own their homes while ensuring that private landlords are not unfairly expropriated.

Between 1918 and 1980, owner-occupation grew largely at the expense of private rental. But for the last 20 years, private rental has been growing at the expense of owner occupation. We saw in chapter 1 that the reasons private rental dwindled in the twentieth century had to do with tight rent controls and security of tenure laws that made it almost impossible for landlords to regain vacant possession of their properties. Conversely, the reasons for its resurgence since the 1980s lie in the scrapping of rent controls and the introduction of six-month 'shorthold' tenancies. These reforms restored the potential for profitability to the sector, and after BTL mortgage products appeared on the market from the mid-nineties, the surge of money back into private rental began.

In an earlier Civitas report on the future of private renting, Daniel Bentley proposed scrapping shorthold tenancies for all but newly-built properties and returning to indefinite tenancy agreements.[21] The insecurity of six-month leases may not have been a problem when the private rental sector was catering mainly for students and other mobile young adults who were not looking to remain in one place for too long, but nowadays the biggest demographic among private tenants is families with children. These are people with local jobs, whose children are enrolled in neighbourhood schools, yet their landlord could at any time give them two months notice to leave, and at the end of every six or 12-month lease, their rent can be hiked to whatever the market will bear. According to Shelter, 27 per cent of private renters with children have moved at least three times in the last five years.[22]

Bentley recommends that market rents should be freely-agreed at the start of any tenancy, but that after that, rent rises should be limited to the rate of inflation. Provided they observe the terms of their lease, he also proposes that tenants should be allowed to remain in occupation for as long as they want.

He denies that this limited return to rent controls would destroy the profitability of the private rented sector in the way that crude rent freezes did after 1916, and this is probably correct. If rents are freely negotiated at the start of each tenancy, but are then pegged to the CPI, research indicates that landlords would continue to receive a decent return on their capital and that few would sell up or go bust.[23]

His suggestion of an indefinite right of tenure, though, could be damaging. This would effectively tie up landlords' capital investment long-term, and would almost certainly depress the value of their houses by making it impossible to sell with vacant possession. Unless landlords (and lenders who take possession of properties) have a right to terminate tenancies when they wish to sell, this proposal could trigger a stampede out of the sector, as well as encouraging among those who remain a return to Rachman-style practices for winkling out sitting tenants when they want to sell up.[24]

Possibly for these reasons, the Labour Party is less radical in its plans. It recommends moving to three-year tenancies, with initial rents freely negotiated and annual cost of living rent rises after that.[25] Shelter similarly argues for five-year tenancies with inflation-linked rent reviews.[26] Both proposals would allow tenants to terminate their agreement with two months' notice.

Whichever of these proposals we go with, there is clearly a strong case on grounds of fairness alone for extending security of tenure beyond its current six or 12 months. Such a change would also have to be a condition of any move to extend the Right to Buy to the private sector, for without extended tenure security, landlords could terminate a lease before a tenant had been in occupation long enough to qualify for an option to purchase.

Since 2013, the RTB qualifying period for council tenants has been three years (the Blair government had raised it to five). A similar residency qualification also applies to the newly introduced voluntary RTB for housing association tenants. Assuming this same rule were extended to the private rented sector as well, tenants would not be eligible to buy their home from their landlord until they had been in occupation for at least three years. To stop landlords terminating the lease before three years have elapsed (in an attempt to prevent tenants from applying to buy their homes), security of tenure would have to be guaranteed for at least that long. The Shelter proposal for five-year leases would meet this requirement best.

After three years of a five-year tenancy had elapsed, tenants of private landlords would be offered the option to purchase their home at any time in the next two years (i.e. during the remaining period of their tenancy). This would give them five years in total to save for a deposit, during which period their rental outgoings would not rise above the rate of inflation. At the end of five years, · the tenancy would lapse, and if they had not exercised their RTB by then, their eligibility to do so would lapse with it (this would give landlords as well as tenants some predictability).

Like council and housing association tenants, private tenants who exercise their RTB would be entitled to a 35 per cent discount off the market value of the house, up to a maximum currently set at £77,900 outside London and £103,900 in London.[27] The same rules should apply to private sector tenants who wish to buy their homes, but with two important riders.

First, the discount should never be so high as to impose losses on the landlord. In the social rented sector, tenants cannot be given discounts which exceed the amount spent on the property by their landlords in the last 10 years, and discounts in the private sector should similarly be reduced to take account of recent improvements costs incurred by landlords. But in addition to this, the discount should be capped so the price at which the tenant purchases is never lower than the price originally paid for the property by the landlord (including the original transaction costs). This means landlords would never be forced to incur losses on their investments – an important safeguard for recent buy-to-let investors and for those who have bought in more depressed property markets. Without such a cap, existing landlords could be unfairly penalised, and new ones would be unlikely to risk investing at all in the future.

Secondly, the RTB in the private sector should be limited to tenants in properties (including residential conversions) which are at least 25 years old. This would ensure that investors are not deterred from buying new properties to rent out. Landlord purchases of new properties represent an important market for the house building industry – according to Hamptons, more than a quarter of homes bought by landlords are newly-built or new conversions, and it is estimated that 23p in every £1 spent by landlords on property purchases goes into the new homes market.[28] Big financial institutions like pension funds and insurance companies have also begun to invest in new building to rent, and the government is encouraging these trends with £1bn of subsidies to support the construction of up to 10,000 new rental homes.[29] It is important that any reform should not jeopardise all this investment in new construction. Twenty-five years should be a long enough window for any landlord (individual or institutional) who buys a new property to recoup their original investment and make a good profit.[30]

Given the increased property values many landlords have been enjoying as a result of the long, fourth house price boom (as well as the rental income they have been getting), many will today be sitting on assets worth a lot more than they paid for them. Even if a tenant qualifies for a maximum discount of £77,900 (or £103,900 in London), these landlords will still enjoy handsome capital gains if they are obliged to sell. The discounts they would have to offer to their tenants would merely share out some of the windfall gains they have been making over the last decade or two as a result of the exceptional circumstances surrounding the long, fourth house price boom.

Any capital gains that are realised are, of course, taxable. However, landlords compelled to sell at a discount to their tenants could be compensated to some degree through CGT concessions. One possibility is to exempt them from the surcharge on gains raised from the sale of residential properties, which was introduced in the 2016 Budget. More radically, they could be allowed to offset the value of the discount they have given against their CGT liability when they sell, which would substantially reduce their tax liability.[31] The cost to the Treasury of any CGT concession could come out of the £4 billion the government has earmarked for its various housing initiatives intended to stimulate owner occupation (for the current, self-defeating Help to Buy policy would be ended).

If RTB were extended to private tenants, most of the tax penalties which have recently been aimed at BTL landlords could be removed. The stamp duty surcharge on second home purchases (which has generated a number of negative unintended consequences requiring early amendments to the policy) could be scrapped, and the tax relief claimed by landlords on the interest they pay on housing loans could be restored.[32] Our tax system is complicated enough without all this extra fiddling. The Bank of England's new controls on BTL mortgages might also be reviewed.

The main benefit, though, would be the effect on the UK owner-occupation rate. There would be an echo of what happened in the 1950s and 1960s when thousands of small landlords sold out to their sitting tenants. Home ownership would start to rise and (a particular advantage of this policy) the cohort born around 1980 who have been missing out on the opportunity to buy (so-called 'Generation Rent') would be able to make up some of the ground they have lost. Generational inequity would start to be restored.

This policy would not kill off the private rented sector, but it would trim back its growth. Prospective landlords (private as well as institutional) would in future be encouraged to buy new-build properties, for these would be immune from RTB for 25 years (ample time to make a decent return on the initial capital outlay). This would give a boost to new housing supply. But they would tend to steer clear of buying older properties, leaving more of the second-hand market to buyers who wish to live in the property. This should increase the availability of housing for prospective owner-occupiers to buy, and exert a downward pressure on prices. This downward pressure should in turn be reinforced by tenants who have exercised their RTB and who then trade up to take advantage of some of the discount they have been given (as commonly happens with those who buy their council houses). This will bring more properties onto the market at the lower end and should help push these prices down even further.

Stopping future bubbles

Extending the RTB is an essential policy for rectifying the generational inequality which has arisen in the UK housing market. But we should not stop there. It is also essential to tighten financial regulation so we stop house prices in future ballooning away from average earnings as they have done since the turn of the century. This will not be easy.

We have seen that the decline of home ownership rates in Britain is the consequence of a much wider set of interlinked housing, planning, demographic and macro- and micro-economic changes. The high cost of house purchase is at the heart of the problem, but this is linked to the way we regulate the financial services industry, the level of interest rates set by the Bank of England, the stagnation in average earnings over the last 15 years, the stickiness of the land use planning system, the way we subsidise the purchasing costs of first-time buyers, rising levels of immigration, the increased popularity of rental housing as an investment, the attraction of London to overseas investors, the continuing growth of single-person households, and much else besides. This complexity makes it very difficult to isolate specific policies that might reduce prices and boost home ownership. Indeed, changing one factor could spark unintended and unwelcome changes in others, for different factors interact with each other in ways that are not always consistent or even predictable.[33]

A further problem is that housing policy forms an integral part of economic policy as a whole, so any significant change is likely to have implications for the whole UK economy. In 2014, the total value of all UK dwellings was estimated at £4.43 trillion, which is 58 per cent of the entire wealth of the country.[34] Housing is the principal form of wealth for most households, and mortgage debt is the main asset class on most banks' balance sheets.[35] Shifting house prices therefore have huge potential implications for consumer demand and credit supply across the whole economy. When we start fiddling with the economics of the housing market, we are also twiddling the knobs on the rest of the economy.

One crucial implication of this is that, while young buyers clearly need house prices to fall, many other people have an interest in ensuring they do not. We have seen that house prices have remained at an impossibly high level since 2008 largely because the government and the Bank of England have maintained record low interest rates in order to avert a deep recession. A rate hike would undoubtedly help bring house prices down by dampening down demand – which is what is needed. But no politician wants to trigger a slump in the housing market while they are in office, for not only would existing owners with big mortgages be badly hit, but any significant increase in interest rates would threaten to choke off the faltering recovery in the wider economy.

This means that even though we can identify one of the main causes of the problem of high house prices (low interest rates), it is difficult to devise a strategy to change it because the knock-on effects for the wider economy of a substantial fall in house prices would be too devastating for any politician or central banker to contemplate.[36] The former director of housing at the Housing Corporation, Matt Leach, captures the dilemma perfectly:

> The problem is the extent of the asset bubble that's been created around land in the UK and particularly in the South of England is such that it cannot easily or quickly be unwound – so much of it is linked to the health of our banks, and to individuals' long term financial security. There is no way of addressing this problem in the short run – housing officials and ministers are operating within almost impossible constraints, which pushes them into short termism. It's easier to announce another

package of 'help for hard pressed homebuyers' than to seriously address chronic issues of undersupply and affordability. They can't deal with the long term strategic stuff.[37]

Nobody in government or anywhere else currently has a clue how to get interest rates back up to normal levels without the whole economy seizing up, so there is not much point suggesting it.[38]

One proposal that might be feasible, however, would be to commit the Bank of England and its Financial Policy Committee (FPC) to meeting a medium-term house price inflation target or band, in addition to its CPI target. This would not necessarily involve interest rate changes; it could be done by manipulating lending criteria. For example, if average house prices threaten to race ahead of average earnings, the Bank might insist on lenders securing bigger deposits from borrowers, limiting their periods of repayment, and toughening affordability tests for those applying for loans. It could also make BTL lending more expensive, and it could force lenders to discriminate against borrowing for the purchase of real estate by increasing the risk weighting attached to these loans (which would reduce the number of such loans they could offer).[39]

When he was governor of the Canadian central bank, the current Governor of the Bank of England pursued policies just like these in an explicit strategy to dampen down house price inflation, and in 2014, the FPC introduced mortgage restrictions here in response to signs that the housing market was starting to over-heat again.[40] But we need more than ad hoc controls. In his recent analysis of the problems which unrestricted credit for house purchases creates in modern capitalist economies, Adair Turner, former chairman of the Financial Services Authority, concludes: 'To achieve a less credit-intensive and more stable economy, we must deliberately manage and constrain lending against real estate assets.'[41]

The Treasury is currently in the process of giving the Bank powers to direct lenders on their loan-to-value and debt-to-income lending criteria (until now it has only been able to demand explanations from lenders who fail to comply with its guidance), and this will strengthen the Bank's armoury.[42] Regulatory powers like these could form the basis for a new statutory requirement on the Bank to meet house price inflation targets which would be achieved by constraining (or loosening) the lending rules governing credit for house purchases in response to fluctuations in national (and perhaps also regional) house prices.

The lesson of the last 20 years is that we can no longer afford simply to target general inflation via interest rate policy while ignoring house price inflation. The Bank already has a statutory duty to keep general inflation at or around two per cent; there should be a corresponding statutory duty to stop house price inflation from spiralling ahead of earnings.

Summary of recommendations

The fourth house price boom started in the late 1990s and, unlike the previous three, has never really ended. Some people – particularly older, established home owners and up to two million new landlords – have made small fortunes as a result of this inflation. But it has left us with a legacy of unaffordable housing, bloated housing debts, gross generational inequity and a falling rate of home ownership that shows no sign of bottoming out.

It is a daunting task to begin to put all this right. In the long term, house prices will have to come down in real terms, and probably in money terms too, for real earnings are hardly rising. Lending has to tighten, and we have to dampen down the new sources of demand (especially buy-to-let purchases) which have been propping up the over-inflated housing market since the turn of the century. As at the end of the third house price boom in the early nineties, such adjustments will be painful. But (to quote a former prime minister) there really is now no alternative. The market has been stretched as tight as it can possibly bear. There is nowhere else for it to go now but down.

Whether we can ever get back to the sort of conditions we enjoyed before the fourth boom got going – an affordable average house price to average earnings multiple below four, positive real interest rates of two or three per cent, and a home ownership rate of around 70 per cent trending upwards – is anybody's guess (in London it already looks well nigh impossible). But this is where we should be aiming. With that in mind, we should commit ourselves to the following five policies as our first steps to restoring our nation of home owners (they should be seen as a package, not a series of discrete options):

1 End all current demand-side government subsidies which claim to make home ownership more affordable by giving first-time buyers loans, grants, savings supplements, tax concessions or mortgage guarantees. These policies are not only wasteful of public money; they end up making a bad situation even worse by inflating prices even higher.

2   Introduce a statutory duty on the Bank of England to regulate mortgage lending to keep the ratio of average house prices to average earnings within a specified range over the medium term. The upper end of this range may need to be set high initially (given the existing level of house prices) but should gradually be reduced to no more than the historical limit to affordability (probably a ratio no higher than 4.5:1).

3   Rectify the generational inequality in access to home ownership by extending the statutory Right to Buy currently enjoyed by tenants in the social rented sector to tenants of landlords in the private sector. Similar rules of eligibility and rates of discount should apply, although discounts should be capped to prevent the possibility of landlords incurring losses, and the RTB should not apply to properties less than 25 years old. Landlords should be partially compensated by CGT concessions when they sell. The standard duration of tenancies in the private sector should be extended to five years to prevent landlords from terminating leases before tenants have achieved the residential qualification period required to activate the RTB.

4   Consistent with other government objectives, and within the limits of the legal competency of the government, reduce net immigration to reduce mounting pressure on the housing market; legislate to prohibit non-UK citizens from buying residential property here; and over time, return stamp duty on residential property sales to its 1997 rate (basically, a flat one per cent).

5   Continue to encourage increased rates of new building by easing planning controls and releasing more green belt land, and investigate ways of

compensating residents who live close to new developments with a share of the proceeds from 'planning gain' and/or the tax revenues generated by new development. Such supply-side measures should help stimulate increased construction, although we have to recognise the very limited contribution they can make to delivering lower house prices and an enhanced rate of home ownership.

Notes

Chapter 1 – The end of the home owner revolution?

1   Peter Saunders, *A Nation of Home Owners*, Unwin Hyman, 1990.

2   Daniel Mahoney and Tom Knox, 'What's behind the housing crisis?', Centre for Policy Studies *Economic Bulletin* No.68, 20 November 2015.

3   The HomeOwners' Alliance, 'The Death of a Dream', London, November 2012, p.7.

4   The 10 per cent home ownership figure for 1914 is widely cited in the academic literature. It appears, for example, in Mark Swenarton and Sandra Taylor, 'The scale and nature of the growth of owner occupation in Britain between the wars', *Economic History Review*, vol.38, 1985, 373-92, and is repeated in many sources including 'A Century of Change: Trends in UK statistics since 1900', House of Commons Library (Dec 1999), p.12. However, the Dept for Communities and Local Government recently published an estimate by Alan Holmans suggesting that the home ownership rate in 1919 in England & Wales was as high as 23 per cent (DCLG, Live table on household characteristics, Table 801).

5   Alan Murie ('The Right to Buy: History and Prospect', History & Policy, Policy Papers, 11 May 2015) gives a figure of 1.8 million. Ben Pattison and his colleagues (Ben Pattison with Diane Diacon and Jim Vine, 'Tenure Trends in the UK Housing System', Building and Social Housing Foundation, 2010) say it is over two million, although the rate of sales has slowed to a dribble since 2003. As a result of these sales and the sharp reduction in new council building since 1979, council housing as a proportion of the nation's total housing stock fell from 27 per cent in 1980 to just 11 per cent in 2003 (Daniel Chandler and Richard Disney, 'Housing market trends and recent policies' in Carl Emmerson, Paul Johnson and Helen Miller (eds), 'IFS Green Budget', 2014, Institute of Fiscal Studies, February 2014, p.123).

6   In 1986, a new Housing Act raised discounts for flats to between 44 per cent (after two years of tenancy) and 70 per cent (after 15 years). Discounts for houses were 32 per cent after two years'

tenancy, increasing to 60 per cent after 30 years: Murie, 'The Right to Buy'. We shall see in chapter 7 that these rates have changed up and down several times since then. The discount for flats currently starts at 50 per cent.

7   Bernard Clarke, 'Data shows housing tenure trends continuing', Council of Mortgage Lenders press release, 5 March 2015.

8   In his much-discussed book *Capital in the Twenty-first Century* (Belknap Press, 2014), Thomas Piketty refers to 'this vast group, where individual wealth ranges from barely 100,000 euros to more than 400,000' and notes that 'a key role is often played by ownership of a primary residence and the way it is acquired and paid for... Make no mistake: the growth of a true 'patrimonial middle class' was the principal structural transformation of the distribution of wealth in the developed countries in the twentieth century' (p.260: thanks to Daniel Bentley for bringing this passage to my attention).

9   ONS, *Wealth and income* 2014, Table 1 and Figure 4: http://www.ons.gov.uk/ons/dcp171778_368612.pdf

10 Fabrice Murtin and Marco Mira d'Ercole, 'Household wealth inequality across OECD countries: new OECD evidence', OECD Statistics Brief, June 2015, no.21, Figure 2. The US exhibits high wealth inequality, despite a relatively high home ownership rate comparable with that of the UK, but this may reflect the lower level of private pension savings there, as well as the decline in low income owner occupation following the 2008 financial crisis (which was largely caused by reckless mortgage lending to low income households).

11 Viewed as an asset, housing has performed better over the last 30 years than almost any other class of investment. The annual rate of return on gold has been 4.6 per cent; interest on savings has averaged 5.7 per cent; the return on equities with all dividends reinvested has been 9.8 per cent; while house prices have risen at an annual rate of 7.8 per cent, to which 4.3 per cent must be added for annual rental yields (or the imputed use value of the housing for owner-occupiers). See Joel Marsden, 'House prices in London', GLA Economics Working Paper No.72, November 2015.

12 Interestingly, tax relief on mortgage interest payments, which originated as an offset against Schedule A tax, remained unchanged for another three decades as politicians feared the electoral repercussions if they withdrew it.

13 A significant proportion of the wealth accumulated through home ownership is now being spent paying for care in old age – between 30,000 and 50,000 properties each year are being sold

to pay for care (David Willetts, *The Pinch*, London Atlantic Books, 2010, p.249).

14 *A Nation of Home Owners*, p.163.

15 Ivor Crewe, 'The disturbing truth behind Labour's rout', *The Guardian*, 13 June 1983; Gordon Marshall, David Rose, Carolyn Vogler and Howard Newby, 'Class, citizenship and distributional conflict in modern Britain', British Journal of Sociology vol.36, 1985, 259-82.

16 I can find no analysis of whether voting shifted due to this policy promise. According to YouGov, the Conservatives enjoyed a lead among outright owners, mortgage-payers and private tenants, but Labour had a 25 point lead among social tenants: https://yougov.co.uk/news/2015/06/08/general-election-2015-how-britain-really-voted/

17 Nigel Keohane and Nida Broughton, 'The Politics of Housing', Social Market Foundation, 2014, p.61.

18 'Homeowners are powerful politically at the national level and at the local level', Nigel Keohane and Nida Broughton, 'The Politics of Housing', p.5.

19 Taxing the imputed rental income of home owners meant that expenses incurred in generating this 'income' – notably the interest payments on housing loans – could be offset against it for tax purposes. After Schedule A tax was abolished on people's first homes, mortgage interest tax relief continued as an expensive anachronism for another twenty years – further testimony to the voting power of home owners.

20 Andrew Grice, 'Budget 2015: George Osborne to raise levels for inheritance tax in first Tory-only Budget', *The Independent*, 8 July 2015.

21 The latest in a long line of sociological theories of Britain's class structure identifies at the top an 'elite' class of CEOs, directors, barristers and the like who are high in economic, social and cultural capital. According to the authors: 'Our findings clearly demonstrate the power of a relatively small, socially and spatially exclusive group at the apex of British society' (Mike Savage et al., 'A new model of class' *Sociology*, vol.47, 2013, p.234).

22 All cited in *A Nation of Home Owners*, p.59.

23 James Chapman, '"We'll create a job for everyone that wants one": Cameron pledges to create highest employment rate in developed world', *Daily Mail*, 31 March 2015.

24 In *A Nation of Home Owners* I reviewed evidence on the possessive traits of very young children, and the psychological

stress created when adults are stripped of their personal possessions. I would add to this the fact that in our evolutionary past, individuals who were happy to share everything would have been exploited by those who kept what they had to themselves and their immediate kin, and their genes would not have survived. See Jonathon Haidt's *The Righteous Mind* (New York, Pantheon Books, 2012).

25 *A Nation of Home Owners*, Table 2.4.

26 The term was popularised by Robert Putnam, 'Bowling Alone: America's Declining Social Capital'. *Journal of Democracy* vol. 6 (1995), pp.65–78.

27 Dan Andrews and Aida Caldera Sánche, 'The Evolution of Homeownership Rates in Selected OECD Countries' *OECD Journal: Economic Studies*, 2011/1, p.211.

28 Data pre-1971 are from Table 1.1 of *A Nation of Home Owners*. Data 1971 onwards computed from Office for National Statistics, *Dwelling stock by tenure* Historical Series, Table 101. Absence of reliable data points between 1914 and 1939 explain the straight trend lines over this early period in the graph.

29 Housing benefit (HB) is a means tested benefit paid to tenants of private and social landlords to help them pay their rent. Since the 1980s, the UK has moved away from subsidising the construction of low-cost rental housing (building council houses to let at below market rents) to subsidising the incomes of low cost renters instead. HB rates are fixed at 30 per cent of local rent levels, so if rents rise faster than wages, the total bill must rise. Economists like Kristian Niemietz and Ryan Bourne believe it doesn't make much difference whether government subsidises producers or consumers of housing, for in both cases large sums of money get spent ensuring that poorer families get a roof over their heads (Ryan Bourne and Kristian Niemietz, 'Smoking out red herrings', Institute of Economic Affairs Briefing 14/04, 2014, p.26). There is, though, a major difference between these two subsidy strategies. Although most of the money spent on HB goes to housing associations, who can use some of their rent revenues to build more stock, more than one-third of it goes to private landlords, most of whom buy existing (often very old) housing stock rather than new (£9.5bn of the £24bn HB bill goes to private landlords – Daniel Bentley, 'The Future of Private Renting', Civitas, 2015). Rather than increasing the supply of new housing, the government therefore now spends almost £10bn every year boosting the incomes of private landlords who then spend the money on other things. Niemietz ('Redefining the Poverty Debate', p.64) tells us that 5 million households – 44 per cent of all renters – now receive HB, and they include

1.7m private sector tenants (up from 771,000 in 2000). The cost to taxpayers is astronomical: HB spending now absorbs £24 billion per annum, one quarter of our budget deficit (Kate Allen, 'UK housing: The £24bn property puzzle', *Financial Times*, 1 June 2015). The government has now capped HB payments in an attempt to wrestle down this total cost, but such measures will have no more than a marginal impact.

30 The National Landlords Association estimates there are 1.4 million landlords in Britain (cited in Brewin Dolphin, 'Is the Buy-To-Let boom over?', *The Spectator* advertising feature, 14 November 2015), although other estimates put the figure higher. 78 per cent of landlords have only one property (David Smith, 'The Home Front', *The Sunday Times*, 15 November 2015).

31 Interestingly, they have fallen in a number of other 'Anglosphere' countries too. In *A Nation of Home Owners* (p.18) I included a table of international owner occupancy rates in the early eighties. New Zealand then had a 72 per cent recorded home ownership rate, and Australia 70 per cent. Both are now below this figure, and the USA is still on 65 per cent, where it was in 1981.

32 A partial exception is the joint report by Shelter and the Resolution Foundation ('Housing in Transition', June 2012) which suggests that owner occupation could increase slightly (from 64 per cent to 65 per cent by 2025) if the economy recovers. If the economy stays weak, however, it predicts a further fall in home ownership to 62 per cent.

33 Source: For EU countries, Michael Neal, 'A cross-country comparison of home ownership rates' (National Association of Home Builders, 'Eye on Housing', 19 June 2015); other countries from Wikipedia.

Chapter 2 – Do people still want to own?

1 Results of the survey reported in Eleanor Taylor, 'Public attitudes to housing in England', Dept for Communities & Local Government, HMSO, 2011.

2 In 1975 the National Economic Development Office reported 69 per cent preferring owner occupation (40 per cent among council tenants). The 1978 General Household Survey found 72 per cent preferring owner occupation (49 per cent among council tenants). In 1986, the Building Societies Association found about three-quarters preferring owner occupation, including almost half of council tenants. *A Nation of Home Owners* p.61.

3   Ben Pattison with Diane Diacon and Jim Vine, 'Tenure Trends in the UK Housing System', Building and Social Housing Foundation 2010.

4   The average age of women when they have their first child is now 30, and as many women start a family when they are over the age of 35 as under the age of 25. Office for National Statistics, 'Live Births in England and Wales by Characteristics of Mother 1, 2013', 16 October 2014, Figure 1.

5   The growth of the 'sharing economy' might be one indication of a growing disenchantment with private ownership among the young (thanks to Ian Winter for alerting me to this). These trends are more developed in the UK than anywhere else in Europe. See Lauren Davidson 'Mapped: How the sharing economy is sweeping the world' *Daily Telegraph* 23 September 2015.

6   Alison Wallace, 'Public Attitudes to Housing', Joseph Rowntree Foundation 2010, Fig.2.

7   Source: Council for Mortgage Lenders, 'Maturing attitudes to home ownership' *Housing Finance*, Issue 02, June 2012, Tables 1-4.

8   Council for Mortgage Lenders, 'Maturing attitudes to home ownership' p.4.

9   Halifax, 'Five years of Generation Rent', Lloyds Banking Group, 2015, p.2.

10 Qualitative research with young people suggests they see home ownership as desirable but unattainable, and that they express 'universal frustration' about lack of affordability – Kim McKee, 'Young people, home ownership and the fallacy of choice', University of St Andrews Briefing No.6, 20 May 2015, p.2.

11 Halifax, 'Five years of Generation Rent', p.5.

Chapter 3 – The bubble that never burst

1   The Nationwide Building Society estimated the average UK house price in the third quarter of 2015 at £195,733, but this hid huge regional variations. In London it was more than twice the national average at £443,399. The Outer metropolitan (£326,785), Outer South East (£247,286) and East Anglia (£199,334) regions were also above the national average, with all other regions below it. The lowest average house prices were in Northern England (£124,345), Northern Ireland (£127,562) and Scotland (£140,402), with Yorkshire & Humberside, North West England and Wales all around £145,000. Nationwide Building Society, House PriceIndex, *Regional Quarterly Indices.*

2   Arguably, mortgage payments are the equivalent of the rent paid by tenants and should not therefore be deducted (for if owners weren't buying their homes, they would still have to make rental payments). The gross figures are therefore a more appropriate guide to capital gains. The data are set out in detail in *A Nation of Home Owners*, ch.3.

3   Expressed as a real, annual rate of return on their initial investment, median capital gains were the equivalent of a 14 per cent return. This compared very favourably with interest paid on building society savings accounts over this period (between four and 10 per cent) and shares (which rose on average by only four per cent per annum).

4   See, for example, Patrick Collinson, 'Welcome to London, where homes earn more than their earners', *The Guardian*, 17 March 2015.

5   This was a common argument among Marxist housing economists in the 1980s at the time when I was writing *A Nation of Home Owners*. For Clarke and Ginsburg: 'The gain is achieved at the expense of another owner-occupier who purchases the house'; for Jim Kemeny: 'The capital gain... is paid for through higher housing costs for remaining or new owner-occupiers'; and for Michael Ball, home ownership is 'a way of making money for a lucky few at the expense of others' (all quoted on pp.144-45 of my book, and all hopelessly wrong).

6   Sources: Office for National Statistics Year Book and website; Nationwide Building Society *House Price Index*.

7   In Fig. 3a, changes earlier in time appear smaller than those that come later because the lines represent changes in absolute values. By expressing values as their natural logs, exponential rates of growth are flattened out into straight lines, so rates in different time periods can be compared in Fig 3b by comparing the slope of the line.

8   This multiple was similar to that found in other Anglophone countries including the USA, Australia, New Zealand, Canada and Ireland. See Wendell Cox and Hugh Pavletich, *11th Annual Demographia International Housing Affordability Survey 2015* http://www.demographia.com/dhi.pdf

9   In the past, house price booms have generally started in London and the south east, but have later rippled out to the rest of the country which has then (proportionately) caught up. This has not happened in this latest boom, however, where London has widened the gap with the rest of the country (including its southern hinterland). At the turn of the century, average house prices were £140,148 in London, £126,793 in the outer

metropolitan area, and £95,475 in the outer south east. This compared with, for example, £50,606 in the north of England, £57,669 in Yorkshire & Humberside, and £62,829 in Scotland. By the third quarter of 2015, average prices had risen to £443,399 in London (up 216 per cent), compared with £326,785 (158 per cent) in the outer metropolitan area, £247,286 (159 per cent) in the outer south east, £124,345 (146 per cent) in the north, £145,673 (153 per cent) in Yorkshire & Humberside, and £140,402 (123 per cent) in Scotland (data from Nationwide Building Society *House Price Index*). So while Scotland has fallen behind somewhat, the rest of the country has more-or-less been keeping up with the south east, but all areas have fallen way behind London.

10   Wendell Cox and Hugh Pavletich, *11th Annual Demographia International Housing Affordability Survey*, p.20.

11   In some boroughs it is nearer three-quarters. In Hackney, only 26 per cent of households own their homes; in Tower Hamlets 27 per cent; in Islington 29 per cent. Office for National Statistics, *A century of home ownership and renting in England and Wales* 19 April 2013.

12   Kathryn Hopkins, 'House prices forecast to rise by 20 per cent over next five years', *The Times*, 6 November 2015

13   The Halifax price-to-earnings ratio, which averaged 3.64 in the 1980s and 1990s, grew to above 5 before the 2008 crash. By the end of 2014, it was back at 5.07 (Andrew Oxlade, 'House price to earnings ratio points to 19pc fall' *Daily Telegraph* 8 January 2015).

14   'Boom? What boom?' *Financial Times*, 26 November 2015.

15   David Willetts, *The Pinch*, London, Atlantic Books, 2010, pp.72 & 80.

16   And it is predicted that for those born in 1990, the proportion will fall to only 39 per cent. See Neal Hudson 'A crisis of home ownership?' Savills Housing Market Note, 17 July 2015.

17   All these figures are from New Policy Institute, 'A Nation of Renters', May 2015.

18   Source: Bank of England Interactive Data Base, 3996851 (SVR) and 4026730 (Lifetime Tracker).

19   Historically, nominal interest rates on mortgages have ranged between about four per cent and six per cent, except in the 1970s and 1980s when high inflation drove them as high as 14 per cent. The eight per cent nominal rate in the 1990s was therefore historically high given inflation at only two per cent. See Hannah Phaup, *Historical sources of mortgage interest rate statistics*, Bank of England, 1 September 2015, Chart C.

20 Nationwide Building Society, 'Housing Affordability for First Time Buyers'.

21 The Single Variable Rate is the default interest rate charged to borrowers after the term of a special fixed rate mortgage comes to an end. It is higher than most rates offered in the market, and many borrowers therefore switch to a new fixed rate deal when their existing one ends. Tracker mortgages are pegged to the Bank of England base rate for the lifetime of the loan. Before 2008 they were commonly fixed at around 0.5 per cent above base rate, although some were fixed at or even below it. Since base rate dropped to 0.5 per cent following the 2008 global financial crisis, most tracker mortgages have been fixed at around 2 per cent above it.

22 Nigel Keohane and Nida Broughton, 'The Politics of Housing', Social Market Foundation, 2014, p.43.

23 Spain, Ireland and the USA all experienced huge increases in house prices from the late nineties onwards, but all saw sharp reversals after 2008 – unlike Britain which now represents an 'extreme outlier' (Kristian Niemietz, 'Redefining the Poverty Debate', London, Institute of Economic Affairs, 2012, p.58). Part of the explanation may be that these three countries all saw a huge increase in the rate of new building as prices rose, whereas in Britain, new construction was more sluggish. When the crash came, they therefore had much more unsold stock, which meant prices fell more dramatically than in Britain (Tejvan Pettinger, *UK house price to income ratio and affordability*, blog 5568, 21 September 20015, www.economicshelp.org). In Ireland, 700,000 new homes were built in just 10 years. When the crash came in 2008, house prices plummeted 50 per cent.

24 In the 1990s the Clinton administration pushed US lenders to advance more loans to low income ('sub-prime') home buyers, accusing them of discriminating against ethnic minorities. This led to a relaxation of the normal lending rules, and millions of poorly-secured loans were advanced. These were then packaged as 'securities' and sold on the US and international markets to realise funds that could be used for more lending. When the loans went bad, many western banks were left holding billions of pounds of worthless assets. See Johan Norberg, *Financial Fiasco*, Washington, Cato Institute, 2009, chapter 2.

25 Ever since the Great Depression of the 1930s, central bankers have sought to stimulate the economy by cutting interest rates. However, most bank lending in the advanced economies today is used to buy property, not to invest in new productive activity. In 1928, 30 per cent of all bank loans in 17 advanced economies went into property; by 2007 it was almost 60 per cent.

The former head of Britain's Financial Services Authority, Adair Turner, warns that this shift means that interest rate cuts today run a high risk of creating speculative property bubbles ('The financial crisis, Fresh thoughts: A British regulator on the financial crisis', *The Economist*, 14 November 2015) This is exactly what happened in Britain after 2008.

26 The IFS notes that it is these record low interest rates which have kept the rate of repossessions much lower than it was in the early 1990s, when the previous boom crashed. Chris Belfield, Daniel Chandler and Robert Joyce, 'Housing: Trends in prices, costs and tenure', Institute of Fiscal Studies Briefing Note 161, February 2015, p.14.

27 At this point, the generational inequity started to reverse a little as older savers received negative real interest on their deposits while younger borrowers paid little or no real interest on their mortgage loans.

28 In strict economic parlance, we are told the current (post-2008) house price boom does not constitute a 'bubble' because it is not being driven by speculative activity motivated by a belief that prices will keep rising (Daniel Chandler and Richard Disney, 'Housing market trends and recent policies' in Carl Emmerson, Paul Johnson and Helen Miller (eds) *IFS Green Budget 2014*, Institute of Fiscal Studies, 5 February 2014). However, the authors of this report are only talking about the period since 2008. They accept that there was a 'bubble' in the early years of this century, but they think the price reduction after 2008 deflated it, and their analysis therefore compares current prices to their previous peak in 2007. In my view, however, we are still in a long price boom which was only temporarily interrupted by the 2008 financial crisis. As Fig.2 makes clear, it is still a tightly over-stretched market and the 2008 correction did not drive prices down to anywhere near their historic trend level. Prices today keep rising (fuelled by ultra-low borrowing costs) far in excess of historic earnings:prices multiples. This looks very much like a continuing bubble, and it seems destined to burst.

29 Rising house prices tend to crowd out more productive investment as a greater proportion of borrowing gets diverted into property (Angus Armstrong, *UK housing market: problems and policies*, p.F6). This has been happening at a time when the wider economy is in need of more infrastructure spending, more investment in R & D, and more spending on apprenticeships and training.

30 The Halifax price-to-earnings ratio went above 5 in December 2014. This was far above the long-term average of 4.1,

suggesting that prices were 19 per cent over-valued. In the 1980s and 1990s, however, the ratio averaged only 3.64, so if that is taken as the base line, prices by 2015 were 28 per cent over-valued. Andrew Oxlade, 'House prices to earnings ratio points to a 19pc fall – but is the measure flawed?' *Daily Telegraph*, 8 January 2015.

31 A reduction from a median multiple of 4.9 to one of 2.9. Ryan Bourne, 'Low pay and the cost of living', Institute of Economic Affairs Briefing 14/05, September 2014, p.32.

32 Estimate by Whittaker, cited by Daniel Chandler and Richard Disney, 'Housing market trends and recent policies', p.107.

33 Halifax figures, cited by Philip Aldrick, 'The Bank of England must take a measure of Carney's Canadian tonic', *The Times*, 6 February 2016.

34 In June 2014 the Financial Policy Committee of the Bank of England recommended that lenders should limit the number of new residential mortgages involving loan-to-income ratios of 4.5 or higher to no more than 15 per cent of all their lending. It also suggested that all new mortgage applications should be subjected to a 'stress test' assessing if borrowers could repay at three per cent higher than the existing mortgage rate. Following this advice, many lenders imposed their own loan-to-income restrictions, mostly at between four and five, and particularly targeted at first-time buyers and smaller borrowers. Bank of England, *UK Housing Market*, 4 July 2015 (Powerpoint presentation)

35 Office of National Statistics, *Housing and home ownership in the UK* ONS Digital, January 22 2015. Geoffrey Meek notes that existing owners trading up to more expensive properties have also increased the size of their deposits, from an average of 31 per cent of the purchase price in 1988 to 39 per cent in 2009, but this is a much smaller rise than that experienced by first-time buyers. First-time buyers today are therefore expected to supply deposits much closer to what existing owners can afford, yet the latter have access to the capital gains made on their current home. 'A long-run model of housing affordability', *Housing Studies* vol.26, 2011, p.1097.

36 Eleanor Lawrie, 'The 100 year club', *This is Money*, 7 September 2015: http://www.thisismoney.co.uk/money/mortgageshome/article-3222157/Professions-100-years-save-deposit-buy-home.html

37 For the 15 years prior to the 2008 financial crisis, private sector rents were rising in line with average earnings, although house

prices and mortgage costs were rising much faster - Ben Pattison with Diane Diacon and Jim Vine, *Tenure trends in the UK housing system* Building and Social Housing Foundation 2010.

Chapter 4 – Is tight supply the main problem?

1   'Increases in house prices relative to incomes have probably been at least partly responsible for a significant decline in homeownership (and a rise in private renting) since the early 2000s, reversing the trend seen over the late 20th century' Chris Belfield, Daniel Chandler and Robert Joyce, 'Housing: Trends in prices, costs and tenure', Institute of Fiscal Studies Briefing Note 161, February 2015, p.2.

2   Neal Hudson, 'The value of land', Housing Market Note, 4 June 2015, Savills Residential Research.

3   Ben Pattison with Diane Diacon and Jim Vine, 'Tenure Trends in the UK Housing System'.

4   Source: Dept of Communities & Local Government https://www.gov.uk/government/statistical-data-sets/live-tables-on-dwelling-stock-including-vacants, Table 101. Population figures from Office for National Statistics *Census, Population and Household Estimates.*

5   Brian Green, 'Is the deep-seated problem of housing supply really just about planning?' Brickonomics 19 May 2014: http://brickonomics.building.co.uk/tag/property-transactions/

6   In the short term, this means housing supply is 'relatively fixed' and an increase in demand will lead directly to a rise in the average price level (Chris Belfield, Daniel Chandler and Robert Joyce, *Housing:* 'Housing: Trends in prices, costs and tenure', Institute of Fiscal Studies Briefing Note 161, February 2015, p.7). The influential Barker Review of the issues underlying lack of supply in the UK housing market acknowledged this: 'New supply only accounts for one per cent of the housing stock, and so even measures which change new supply significantly would not have much effect on prices' (Kate Barker, *Review of Housing Supply Final Report*, HMSO, March 2004, p.4).

7   Dept of Communities and Local Government https://www.gov.uk/government/statistical-data-sets/live-tables-on-house-building, Table 241.

8   Kate Barker, *Review of Housing Supply Final Report*, p.5. To bring annual price rises down to 1.8 per cent would take 70,000 extra units each year. The report also recommended an increase of 17,000 pa in social housing construction to meet existing demand, plus another 9,000 to make inroads into the backlog.

9   Michael Lyons, *Mobilising across the nation to build the houses our children need* (The Lyons Housing Review), The Labour Party, 2014.

10 Alan Holmans, 'New estimates of housing demand and need in England, 2011 to 2031', Town & Country Planning Association, *Tomorrow Series, Paper 16*, 2013.

11 Sarah Heath, 'Housing demand and need (England)', House of Commons Library Standard Note, SN06921, 23 June 2014.

12 National Planning and Housing Advice Unit, 'Developing a target range for the supply of new homes across England', NPHAU, 2007; Sarah Health 'Housing need and demand (England)'.

13 CBI, 'Housing Britain: Building new homes for growth', CBI, 2014.

14 The HomeOwners' Alliance, 'The Death of a Dream', London, November 2012.

15 Neal Hudson, 'New build supply: A panacea?' www.pieria.co.uk/articles/new_build_supply_a _panacea

16 Shortly after the Barker Review was published, the government commissioned a group of housing economists to construct a model to predict how much new housing would be needed in the different regions of the country to deliver affordable housing. Their report confirmed that 'as a matter of accounting identity, the number of newly created homes must equal the number of newly forming households' (Office of the Deputy Prime Minister, 'Affordability Targets: Implications for Housing Supply' 2005, p.26). However, they went on to suggest that Barker was still correct to argue that more housing was needed because housing demand is not the same as housing need. In particular, they justified increasing supply on the grounds that it would enable people to buy better quality housing (because prices would fall making higher quality stock more affordable).

17 The two often get elided. For example: 'The fundamental cause of the housing crisis is a severe shortage of homes, pushing up house prices and making them increasingly unaffordable for the majority. The shortage is the inevitable consequence of building too few houses for decades, meaning the UK has consistently failed to provide enough homes for its burgeoning population', HomeOwners' Alliance, 'The Death of a Dream', p.16.

18 'There is only one statistic in which the UK is clearly an international outlier, and that is the completion rate of new dwellings over time... UK completion rates show much less year-on-year variation, and a much lower long-term average... Housing supply in the UK has become completely unresponsive

to demand', Kristian Niemietz, 'Redefining the Poverty Debate', Institute of Economic Affairs, 2012, pp.85-6.

19 Kate Allen, 'UK housing: The £24bn property puzzle', *Financial Times*, 1 June 2015.

20 Daniel Chandler and Richard Disney, 'Housing market trends and recent policies'. See also: *The Economist* 'Through the roof', 26 September 2015.

21 Nigel Keohane and Nida Broughton, 'The Politics of Housing', Social Market Foundation, 2014.

22 Department for Communities and Local Government, *The Calcutt Review of housebuilding delivery*, 2007.

23 "Having a stock of land helps a homebuilder cope with fluctuations in the housing market and also helps to reduce its exposure to risk resulting from the planning system. We have not found any evidence that homebuilders have the ability to anti-competitively hoard land or own a large amount of land with planning permission on which they have not started to build. Apart from the homebuilding firms, the available information suggests that the largest 'landbank' may be that held by the public sector. Homebuilders are, to some extent, constrained by the availability of suitable land." Office for Fair Trading, *Homebuilding in the UK*, 2008, p.6.

24 'The weight of evidence seems to point to the causal links running from market demand to planning approvals and then, inevitably, to the supply of new homes. The more demand in the market, the more house builders seek planning permissions, the more they build. This, at face value, seems to dilute the strength of the widely-held view that the supply of new homes is limited by the planning system.' Brian Green, 'Is the deep-seated problem of housing supply really just about planning?'

25 Data sourced from Neal Hudson, *The value of land*, Fig.2. At the time of the 2008 crash there were mounting concerns (particularly from small and medium sized builders) about shortage of development finance as the banks starved companies of borrowing. But by 2015, planning restrictions and land shortages were again the leading complaints. Concern is also expressed about shortages of skilled labour – one recruitment agency estimates that Britain is short of 100,000 carpenters, 89,000 plumbers and 27,000 bricklayers (Alistair Osborne, 'Can we build it? No we can't', *The Times*, 3 December 2015).

26 Martin Wolf, 'Britain's self-perpetuating property racket', *Financial Times*, 8 January 2015.

27 The HomeOwners' Alliance, 'The Death of a Dream'.

28 The 'Gross Development Value' of a site is calculated by multiplying the current price of comparable houses in the area by the number of houses that can be built on the plot. Subtract the cost of the development (labour and materials) and a margin for profit, and the result is the maximum price the developer will be willing to pay the landowner. See Neal Hudson, *The value of land.*

29 Compulsory purchase is possible where land is required 'to carry out a function which Parliament has decided is in the public interest' (Dept for Communities & Local Government, 'Compulsory purchase and compensation', Office of the Deputy Prime Minister, London, October 2004, para 1.8). Statutory bodies such as the Highways Authority and local councils, as well as public utilities, have CPO powers which can be used to buy land designated for new roads or other major infrastructure projects, as well small sites needed for, say, electricity pylons. Development corporations established by statute – e.g. new town corporations, or the Olympic Authority charged with redeveloping East London in preparation for the 2012 Games – can also buy land compulsorily and use it for new housing development. According to Jamie Ratcliffe (*The homes London needs*, Policy Exchange, 2016), local authorities can also issue CPOs for new housing development, but only if planning consent is already in place and swift delivery of new housing can be guaranteed. He warns that use of CPOs to get more housing built can be time-consuming and expensive (for compensation is determined by the intended use value, not the existing use value of the land).

30 Recently, planning consents have risen relative to new housing starts, but developers can still only build if they believe they can sell at a price based on what they paid for the land. This helps explain why there are so many plots with planning permission that nevertheless remain undeveloped. In 2013, there were permissions outstanding for 381,390 new homes, but only 134,110 were started (in London the figures are even more stark: as of early 2014, planning permissions were outstanding on 172,000 private sector homes across 766 sites, but there were only 15,790 starts by private developers in the twelve months that followed).These data were compiled by Daniel Bentley of Civitas using statistics from the ONS, the Local Government Association and the Office of the Mayor of London, and are reproduced here with his permission.

31 Neal Hudson, 'Land for new homes', Savills Housing Market Note, 14 August 2015.

32 The acronym was first used in the 1980s by the Conservative Secretary of State for the Environment, Nicholas Ridley to refer to local groups whose position on any development proposal is: Not In My Back Yard. It is still in widespread usage today as a term of abuse for those obstructing new developments.

33 *The Economist*, 'Through the roof', 26 September 2015.

34 *The Economist* magazine is just one of a number of influential voices arguing that the major cause of the crisis of housing affordability is over-restrictive planning controls: 'Britain's Byzantine, murky planning system makes housing supply unresponsive to demand ... Until that changes, efforts to deflate the housing bubble will not get far.' 'Housing: Giving and taking' *The Economist* 28 November 2015.

35 Wendell Cox and Hugh Pavletich, 11th *Annual Demographia International Housing Affordability Survey*.

36 Christian Hilber and Wouter Vermeulen, 'The impact of supply constraints on house prices in England' *The Economic Journal*, vol.124, June 2014.

37 P.34. Having said that, Hilber and Vermuelin find that shortage of development land was not a major factor in driving up house prices over the last 35 years except in a relatively small number of highly urbanised areas.

38 Dept for Communities & Local Government, *National Planning Policy Framework*, March 2012: http://planningguidance. communities.gov.uk/wp-content/themes/planning-guidance/ assets/NPPF.pdf

39 The CBI complains that 'many house builders do not encounter the promised pro-growth mentality at local level' (*Housing Britain: Building new homes for growth* CBI 2014, p.23). See also Szu Ping Chan, 'Three reasons why Britain's housing market is broken', *Daily Telegraph*, 22 September 2014.

40 Daniel Mahoney and Tom Knox, 'What's behind the housing crisis?'

41 Christopher Hope, 'Thousands of new homes on green belt in biggest shake-up for 30 years' *Daily Telegraph* 8 December 2015. Starter homes are sold to first-time buyers under the age of 40 at a 20 per cent discount. Prices are capped at £250,000 outside London, and £450,000 in London. We discuss this policy in chapter 6.

42 'The housing market: can we fix it?', *The Economist*, January 16 2016.

43 Ryan Bourne and Kristian Niemietz, 'Smoking out red herrings', Institute of Economic Affairs Briefing 14/04, 2014.

44   Bourne notes that in the south-east of England, agricultural land
      with permission for residential development is often worth at
      least one hundred times more than comparable land without it
      (Ryan Bourne, 'The UK doesn't need more social housing', *Daily
      Telegraph*, 21 January 2016). Another estimate from 2007 suggests
      that a hectare of agricultural land in the south-east was selling
      for £7,410 while residential land was selling for £3.32 million
      (Leunig, cited by Niemietz, p.87).

45   Section 106 of the 1990 Town and Country Planning Act allows
      planners to include provision for 'planning gain' when granting
      permission for new development. Over the years, various
      attempts have been made by governments to 'capture' some of
      the increased value of land that follows when planning
      permission is granted. A 100 per cent Betterment Charge was
      introduced under the 1947 Act, but repealed in 1953, and an 80
      per cent Development Land Tax was introduced in 1975 and
      scrapped ten years later. In 2004 the Barker Report proposed a
      'Planning Gain Supplement (see Anthony Andrew, Michael Pitt
      and Matthew Tucker, 'The evolution of betterment in the United
      Kingdom' Journal of Retail and Leisure Property (2007) vol 6,
      273–280). This would be a levy on landowners at the point when
      land is given planning permission. Provided the tax was not set
      at too high a level, Barker optimistically suggested that this
      should not discourage owners from selling their land for
      development, nor push up house prices, but this has not been
      the experience with the betterment and development taxes
      levied in the past. The Labour Party's Lyons inquiry also
      advocated 'capturing' the increased value of land produced by
      planning permission and using it to fund infrastructure for new
      developments (p.10). But the basic problem remains that taxes
      like these can destroy the incentive for landowners to sell.
      Today, local planners generally content themselves with
      negotiating with developers to include a 'social' element in their
      plans. Windfall profits that follow planning permission for new
      development are subject only to Capital Gains Tax (which
      applies to all assets, not just development land).

46   Kristian   Niemietz,   'Unaffordable   housing: Causes,
      consequences and solutions', *Intergenerational Foundation* blog,
      11 March 2015: http://www.if.org.uk/archives/6097/housing-
      blog-week-kristian-niemietz-unaffordable-housing-causes-cons
      equences-and-solutions

47   Wendy Wilson, *The New Homes Bonus Scheme*, House of
      Commons Library SN/SP/5724, 6 March 2015. Because new
      housing development increases council tax revenues, local
      authorities can find themselves penalised by reductions in

central government grant. The New Homes Bonus was intended to counteract this and encourage local planning authorities to allow more development in their areas. However, in 2013 the Public Accounts Committee found no evidence that the Bonus was encouraging new housing developments in areas of greatest need.

48 Niemietz suggests that, in return for keeping these tax receipts, local councils should then be required to pick up at least part of the cost of housing benefit payments to low income tenants in their areas (so that if councils prevent new development, they have to pay some of the cost this generates in higher rents). There is, however, a major problem with devolving tax receipts in this way, for different areas of the country vary widely in their potential revenue bases and the demands made on them for services. The reason such a high proportion of local council budgets comes from central grants is precisely because central government tries to ensure that the poorest areas of the country can balance their low revenue streams and high outgoings. The more we allow councils to keep receipts from development in their areas, the more we will exacerbate existing geographical inequalities between richer areas (where most development is likely to occur) and poorer ones (where most of the HB claims will be located). Having said that, however, the government has already moved to allow councils to retain business rate revenues from new developments in their areas, so the principle of central government grant equalisation is already eroding – Paul Johnson, 'Get ready for Osborne's town hall revolution' *The Times*, 8 December 2015.

49 Ryan Bourne proposes that local councils be allowed to experiment with different ways this might be achieved - Ryan Bourne, 'Low pay and the cost of living', p.32. The CBI similarly suggests a system of 'direct compensation for existing home owners whose property values may be negatively affected by new development' (CBI, *Housing Britain: Building new homes for growth*, CBI 2014, p.24).

50 Lyons, p.8.

51 Matt Griffith and Pete Jefferys, 'Solutions for the housing shortage', Shelter, July 2013, p.10 (see also Kate Allen, 'UK housing: The £24bn property puzzle', *Financial Times* 1 June 2015). The right-of-centre think tank, Policy Exchange, has also recently advocated greater use of CPO powers in London, arguing that London's Mayor should be empowered to buy non-residential land or premises which have been out of use for two years or more, paying only existing use value, so more affordable housing can be built. Jamie Ratcliffe, 'The homes

London needs'.

52   Gordon Gemmill, 'Low interest rates allow speculative demand to drive house prices' letter to *Financial Times*, 14 December 2015.

53   Geoffrey Meek, 'A long-run model of housing affordability', *Housing Studies*, vol.26, 2011, 1081-1103.

54   Kristian Niemietz notes that residential floor space per household is lower in Britain than in any other western European country. See Niemietz, 'Danny Dorling's "All that is solid": The worst book on the housing crisis so far', 4 July 2014, IEA Blog.

55   While the population grew by 15 per cent between 1971 and 2011, the number of households grew by 42 per cent, which is roughly in line with the growth of housing stock. Chris Belfield, Daniel Chandler and Robert Joyce, 'Housing: Trends in prices, costs and tenure', Institute of Fiscal Studies Briefing Note 161, February 2015, p.17. Average household size has stopped falling since 2000, partly because the growth in single person and lone parent households has slowed, and partly because housing affordability has tightened.

56   Quoted in Angus Armstrong, 'Commentary: UK housing market problems and policies', *National Institute Economic Review*, no.235, February 2016, p.F4. At any one time, some properties will be vacant and others will be uninhabitable, so it is necessary foe the number of units to be greater than the number of households.

57   www.economist.com/blogs/dailychart/2011/11/global-house-prices

58   OECD, Focus on house prices, 2016 www.oecd.org/eco/outlook/focusonhouseprices.htm

59   Katharina Knoll, Moritz Schularick and Thomas Steger, 'No Price Like Home: Global House Prices, 1870 – 2012' Centre for Economic Policy Research, Discussion Paper 10166, 2015, figure 16. These data would appear to contradict Kriatian Niemietz's claim that Britain's 'housing cost explosion has no parallel in any comparable country' (*Reducing poverty through policies to cut the cost of living* Joseph Rowntree Foundation, June 2015, p.8).

60   Tejvan Pettinger, 'Irish property market, boom and bust', March 2013: http://www.economicshelp.org/blog/7334/economics/irish-property-market-boom-and-bust/

61   Adair Turner, *Between Debt and the Devil*, Princeton University Press 2016, p.65.

62   'By 1970, England and Wales had a crude housing surplus...by the early 1980s, Britain had sufficient housing to meet the needs

of a relatively slow-growing population' Nigel Keohane and Nida Broughton, 'The Politics of Housing', Social Market Foundation, 2014, p.34.

63 Daniel Mahoney and Tim Knox, 'What's behind the housing crisis?' Centre for Policy Studies *Economic Bulletin*, No.68, 20 November 2015. Some commentators deny that the fall in supply of social housing has been a problem, however. Ryan Bourne, for example, points out that Britain's social rented sector is still one of the biggest in Europe, and he cautions against any new expansion ('The UK doesn't need more social housing' *Daily Telegraph* 21 January 2016). In his view, the problem is that restrictive planning laws have stopped private suppliers from meeting the demand created by the decline in social rental.

64 The statistics actually under-estimate the number of new homes being produced because most figures for annual housing output consider only newly-built houses and flats. Total net supply should also include conversions (e.g. houses sub-divided into flats) and changes of use (turning office blocks into flats, shops and pubs into homes, barn conversions). In 2014/15, for example, there were 155.080 newly-built homes, but there were also 20,650 homes created by change of use and 4.950 conversions. Taking account of demolitions, the total housing stock increased by 170,690. Allister Heath, 'Property optimism', *Daily Telegraph*, 13 November 2015.

65 The research, conducted by Christine Whitehead at the LSE, is reported by Kate Allen, 'Housebuilding does not drive down prices, research says', *Financial Times*, 7 June 2015,

66 Geoffrey Meen, 'A long-run model of housing affordability', p.1093.

67 Geoffrey Meen, 'A long-run model of housing affordability', p.1097.

Chapter 5 – New sources of demand

1 The proportion of house sales to 'cash buyers' increased from around 20 per cent in 2005 to more than 35 per cent in 2008, since when it has stayed at or around the 30 per cent level. Most are 'buy-to-let' investors or 'downsizers': Focus Cash Buyers, Hampton International Research, Autumn 2013.

2 For an account of Bank of England inflation indexing, see Ian McAfferty, *Inflation Targeting and Flexibility*, 14 June 2013: http://www.bankofengland.co.uk/publications/Documents/s peeches/2013/speech669.pdf

3   Office for National Statistics *Consumer Prices Indexes: CPI Annual Percentage Change 1989-2015* http://www.ons.gov.uk/ ons/datasets-and-tables/data-selector.html?cdid=D7G7&dataset =mm23&table-id=1.2

4   In a number of speeches before 2008, Brown claimed to have escaped the long British post-war history of stop-go, boom and bust. For details, see: http://www.channel4.com/news/ articles/politics/domestic_politics/factcheck+no+more+boom +and+bust/2564157.html

5   The Treasury and the Bank both followed the economic orthodoxy of the time which held that there was no need to control the creation of credit by bank lending provided the general rate of inflation was being kept low through manipulation of interest rates. Unfortunately, the orthodoxy failed to understand how uncontrolled lending can fuel an asset boom which results in a massive build up of debt which creates increasing instability in the whole economy, even if the general rate of inflation appears to be under control. For a useful discussion of all this, see Adair Turner, *Between Debt and the Devil*.

6   From 92.4 to 105.7: http://www.ons.gov.uk/ons/datasets-and-tables/data-selector.html?cdid=D7BT&dataset=mm23&table-id =1.1

7   David Willetts notes that in December 2004, the Treasury chose to redefine the inflation in the value of people's houses as 'saving behaviour' (at a time when actual household saving was at a record low). Willetts describes this perverse reasoning as 'shockingly complacent' (*The Pinch*, p.78).

8   Buy-to-let investors who already have capital are able to exploit the opportunities offered by record-low interest rates to increase their holdings, but prospective owner-occupiers either cannot afford the high prices or cannot meet the new LTV criteria. Between 2003 and 2013, owner-occupiers with mortgages suffered a net loss of £59bn, while Buy-to-Let landlords made a net gain £434bn. Adair Turner, *Between Debt and the Devil*, pp.123.

9   Economic modelling of housing affordability commissioned by the Department of Communities and Local Government confirms that, 'One of the main reasons why price/earnings ratios worsened in all regions this century was the fall in nominal interest rates' Geoffrey Meen, 'A long-run model of housing affordability', p.1082.

10 The term 'buy-to-let' didn't even exist until 1996. Paragon, 'Eighteen years of buy-to-let', 2014, http://www.paragon-

group.co.uk/file_source/Files/MAIN/pdf/Press per cent20 Releases/2014/18 per cent20Years per cent20of per cent20BTL .pdf

11 The attraction of investment in housing for many individual landlords is the capital gain rather than the income rate of return which averages 3.3 to 3.6 per cent: Ben Pattison with Diane Diacon and Jim Vine, 'Tenure Trends in the UK Housing System', Building and Social Housing Foundation 2010.

12 This compares with £354,500 in stocks and shares, assuming dividends are reinvested – but to make this comparable, we would have to allow for landlords also reinvesting their gains in an expanded portfolio. 'Bricks versus shares', *The Times*, 28 November 2011.

13 Joel Marsden, 'House prices in London', GLA *Economics Working Paper* No.72, November 2015.

14 David Smith, 'On the home front', *The Times*, 15 November 2015.

15 Patrick Hosking, 'Lay off Rigsby, he and his kind are not the cause of the housing crisis', *The Times*, 30 September 2015.

16 Hamptons International, 'The forecast issue', *Market Insight*, Autumn 2015, p.6.

17 National Housing & Planning Advice Unit, 'Buy-to-let mortgage lending and the impact on UK house prices', NHPAU Research Findings, no.1, February 2008, p.14.

18 Hilary Osborne, 'Scrapping buy-to-let tax relief will push rents up, warns lenders' group', *The Guardian*, 20 October 2015.

19 'There will be some properties, where the rental income is high relative to the market value, where buy-to-let borrowers will be able to borrow more than many first time buyers' Rob Thomas, 'Reshaping housing tenure in the UK: the role of buy-to-let', Intermediary Lending Mortgage Association, May 2014, p.16.

20 Applicants must show they can still afford mortgage repayments at 5.5 per cent interest rates, even after paying all the costs of owning the property, including tax liabilities. Harry Wilson and Tom Knowles, 'Lenders get tough over buy-to-let', *The Times*, 30 March 2016.

21 Council of Mortgage Lenders, 'The black and white of buy-to-let: What does the data show?' 8 March 2016: www.cml.org.uk/news/news-and-views/the-black-and-white-of-buy-to-let-what-does-the-data-show/

22 Rob Thomas, 'Reshaping housing tenure in the UK: the role of buy-to-let', p.21.

23 National Housing & Planning Advice Unit, 'Buy-to-let mortgage lending and the impact on UK house prices', NHPAU Research

Findings, no.1, February 2008, p.9.

24 Philippe Bracke, 'Five facts about buy-to-let', *Bank Underground*, 21 July 2015.

25 'Through the roof', *The Economist*, 26 September 2015.

26 Katherine Griffiths, 'Loan surge raises housing bubble fear', *The Times*, 30 September 2015.

27 Andrew Elison, 'Buy-to-let boom as banks ignore warning over risk to economy', *The Times*, 12 November 2015; Katherine Griffiths, 'Buy-to-let could crash the market', *The Times*, 2 December 2015.

28 Quoted by Kathryn Hopkins, 'Stamp duty to rise on purchase of extra homes', *The Times*, 26 November 2015.

29 Anne Ashworth, 'Keep the hard hat George – you'll need it', *The Times*, 26 November 2015.

30 A BTL investor with £80,000 deposit could buy a house for £200,000 with a 60 per cent mortgage. Before the rise, stamp duty gouged £1,500 out of this deposit, but from April 2016 it rose to £7,500. This in turn reduced the size of mortgage that can be taken out, and the price of house that can be purchased falls to £185,000. Merryn Somerset Webb, 'Osborne's tax dabbling can't disguise the mess of public finances', *Financial Times*, 27 November 2015.

31 Philip Aldrick, 'Buy-to-let exodus could spark housing crash, says Bank chief', The Times, 11 November 2015. This may be one reason why BTL properties were not included in the cuts to DGT in the 2016 budget.

32 Andrew Elison, 'Buy to Let landlords poised to sell 500,000 homes in a year', *The Times*, 3 February 2016.

33 Philip Aldrick 'Why selling England by the pound has knocked manufacturing for six', *The Times*, 23 December 2015. This is an issue being addressed in future Civitas publications.

34 Estimate by Property Week, cited in Angus Armstrong, 'Commentary: UK housing market problems and policies' *National Institute Economic Review* no.235, February 2016, F4-F8

35 Chris Papadopoullos, 'UK housing supply shortage makes Britain a hotspot for residential property investors', City A.M., 7 September 2015.

36 Hamptons International, *Focus cash buyers*, Autumn 2013.

37 Tejvan Pettinger, 'UK house price to income ratio and affordability'.

38 Chris Paris, 'The homes of the super-rich', in Iain Hay (ed), *Geographies of the Super Rich* Edward Elgar, 2013.

39 Joel Marsden, 'House prices in London'.

40 Between 2005 and 2015, Halifax reports that London prices more than doubled, compared with a 66 per cent rise in the south and a 36 per cent rise in the north. Kathryn Hopkins, 'Ten years of soaring values widen North-South divide', *The Times*, 11 November 2015.

41 Hamptons International, 'The forecast issue', *Market Insight*, Autumn 2015, p.4.

42 Kate Allen, 'UK housing: The £24bn property puzzle', *Financial Times*, 1 June 2015.

43 'Through the roof' *The Economist* 26 September 2015.

44 David G. Green and Daniel Bentley, 'Finding Shelter', Civitas, 2014.

45 Daniel Chandler and Richard Disney, 'Housing market trends and recent policies' p.109.

46 Research published by the Greater London Authority confirms the growing 'affordability gap' in London. The average London house price is now 10 times median earnings (compared with just 4 times in 1997) and is 5.3 times the average income of those applying for mortgages (the figure in the UK as a whole is 4.4). Joel Marsden, 'House prices in London'.

47 Kathryn Hopkins 'The only way is still up for house prices' *The Times* 9 December 2015.

48 Ian Cowie, 'First timers celebrate as landlords feel the pain' *Sunday Times* 29 November 2015.

49 Bernard Clarke, 'Helping the bank of mum and dad' Council of Mortgage Lenders 5 June 2013, www.cml.org.uk/news/news-and-views/533/

50 Daniel Mahoney and Tim Knox, 'What's behind the housing crisis?'

51 Migration Watch UK, Summary Fact Sheet, MW250, Updated February 2016.

52 Richard Ford, '130,000 new homes needed each year to house migrants' *The Times* 4 December 2015.

53 ONS Digital, 'Housing and home ownership in the UK', Office for National Statistics 22 January 2015.

54 Sarah Heath, 'Housing demand and need (England)', p.12.

55 Alan Holmans, 'New estimates of housing demand and need in England, 2011 to 2031.'

56 Kristian Niemietz, 'Redefining the Poverty Debate', p.83. Niemietz points out that any explanation of Britain's particularly acute problem of housing affordability needs to

focus on factors unique to us. He identifies our restrictive planning regulations, but the explosion in buy-to-let would also seem to meet this criterion (our private rental sector is not bigger than in other comparable countries, where social renting is less developed, but its rate of growth has been exceptional).

Chapter 6 – How government policy is making matters worse

1   Neal Hudson, 'Household Debt', Savills, 29 January 2016.

2   Survey results find 29 per cent supporting financial assistance to first-time buyers, but only 5 per cent supporting allowing developers to build more homes. Nigel Keohane and Nida Broughton, 'The Politics of Housing', Social Market Foundation, 2014, Table 2.

3   Kate Allen, 'UK housing: The £24bn property puzzle', *Financial Times* 1 June 2015.

4   What follows relies heavily on Wendy Wilson and Lizzie Blow, 'Extending home ownership – government initiatives', House of Commons Library , Standard Note SN/SP/3668,.20 March 2015.

5   The government says the scheme is intended to stimulate new building as well as helping buyers with their deposits, and it cites in evidence of its success the 37 per cent increase in new construction that has occurred since Help to Buy was launched.

6   As Chandler and Disney point out, this is rather like a shared ownership scheme in which the government buys up to 20 per cent of the equity and allows people to pay no rent on its share of the equity for the first five years. Daniel Chandler and Richard Disney, 'Housing market trends and recent policies'.

7   Chris Belfield, Daniel Chandler and Robert Joyce, 'Housing: Trends in prices, costs and tenure', Institute of Fiscal Studies Briefing Note 161, February 2015, p.23.

8   Laura Whateley, 'A capital new incentive for Generation Rent in London', *The Times*, 28 November 2015.

9   Daniel Chandler and Richard Disney, 'Housing market trends and recent policies', p.91.

10 Chris Belfield, Daniel Chandler and Robert Joyce, 'Housing: Trends in prices, costs and tenure', p.23.

11 One problem with this scheme is that the 25 per cent payment has to be authorised by a solicitor or conveyancing agent to guard against fraudulent claims, which means buyers will incur

additional professional fees. The maximum subsidy of £3,000 appears almost trivial give that the average price of a starter home bought by first time buyers is now £215,000 (Elizabeth Anderson, 'House prices for first-time buyers rise to record high as supply dwindles' *Daily Telegraph* 13 October 2015). If they have to put down 25 per cent of the purchase price as a deposit, the £3,000 ISA top-up will contribute less than 6 per cent of what they need.

12 There is some uncertainty about how market value will be determined, in order to calculate the 20 per cent discount. See Neal Hudson, 'Starter for Ten' Savills Residential Research Housing Market Note, 19 February 2016.

13 We saw earlier that 'section 106' agreements allow planning authorities to link planning consent to a requirement that developers include some cheap rental housing in new developments for housing associations to buy and let out. The new scheme substitutes affordable homes for sale for homes to rent. See Henry Pryor, 'A plague on all their houses', *The Times* Redbox 12 October 2015: http://www.thetimes.co.uk/redbox/topic/tory-policies/a-plague-on-all-their-houses. At the time of writing, details of how the scheme will work are still being thrashed out between government, developers and lenders. When fully operational, the scheme may be brought under the overall Help to Buy umbrella.

14 'Housing: Giving and taking', *The Economist* 28 November 2015.

15 Jill Sherman, 'First time buyers need to earn £100,000', *The Times*, 19 November 2015.

16 'The Tories' affordable housing plan is a middle class giveaway' *The Economist*, 8 October 2015.

17 Nicholas Watt, 'Shared home ownership scheme to be extended by Tories', *The Guardian*, 7 December 2015.

18 Francis Elliott and Jill Sherman, 'Spending Review', *The Times*, 25 November 2015.

19 Cited in Wendy Wilson and Lizzie Blow, 'Extending home ownership – government initiatives', House of Commons Library.

20 Lisa Bachelor, 'Hundreds of thousands withdraw cash from pension pots after rules relaxation', *The Guardian*, 17 September 2015.

21 Philip Bunn and Alice Pugh, 'Will there really be a pensions spending spree?', Bank underground, 16 October 2015: http://bankunderground.co.uk/2015/10/16/will-there-really-

be-a-pensions-spending-spree/

22 Lucy Warwick-Ching, 'Two-thirds of savers are cashing in pension pots', *Financial Times*, 20 August 2015.

23 Philip Bunn and Alice Pugh, 'Will there really be a pensions spending spree?'

24 Graham Norwood, 'No second chance?', *Sunday Times*, 6 December 2015.

25 Simon French, 'The Help to Buy ISA is economic illiteracy laid bare', *CapX*, 4 November 2015: http://capx.co/the-help-to-buy-isa-is-economic-illiteracy-laid-bare/

26 'Housing: Giving and taking', *The Economist*, 28 November 2015.

27 'The key issue is: is it going to drive up house prices? By and large, in the short run, the answer to that is yes. But in the medium term will the increased house prices stimulate more house building? Our general answer would be probably a bit, but the historical evidence suggests probably not much' (quoted in Wendy Wilson and Lizzie Blow, pp.21-1).

28 Daniel Chandler and Richard Disney, 'Housing market trends and recent policies', p.119.

29 The official evaluation of the scheme makes some heroic assumptions when calculting its impact on house building. It claims that 43 per cent of people buying new homes with equity loans say they would not have been able to afford them if the scheme had not been operating. It then claims that because developers follow demand, this means that the scheme added 43 per cent to new housing output (because each sale results in another new home being built), resulting in a 14 per cent overall increase in new house building since 2013. Stephen Finlay with Peter Williams and Christine Whitehead, 'Evaluation of the Help to Buy Equity Loan Scheme', DGI for Communities and Local Government, February 2016.

30 The interchange is quoted in Wendy Wilson and Lizzie Blow. The Governor of the Bank of England subsequently used the same argument to deny that mortgage guarantees have stoked price inflation. In his letter to the Chancellor in October 2014, the governor of the Bank of England maintains that only 5 per cent of mortgaged house purchases in London between 2007 and 2014 were with the assistance of mortgage guarantees, which indicates that guarantees 'do not appear to have been a material driver' of house price growth. Quoted in Chris Belfield, Daniel Chandler and Robert Joyce, 'Housing: Trends in prices, costs and tenure', p.23.

31 'The ten local authority areas with the highest Help to Buy Equity Loan activity saw median house prices between 2013 and

2014 increase by 6.5 per cent on average. This compares to an increase of 10.5 per cent in median house prices between 2013 and 2014 across England as a whole' Stephen Finlay with Peter Williams and Christine Whitehead, 'Evaluation of the Help to Buy Equity Loan Scheme', p.24.

32 The government's argument is an example of what statisticians refer to as the 'ecological fallacy', where aggregate data at regional level are used to draw inappropriate inferences about individual-level causation. Evidence that average house prices rose more slowly in regions where the take-up of equity loans was higher tells us nothing about whether houses bought with the aid of equity loans inflated in price any slower or faster than other houses.

33 Data taken from Table 3.4 in Stephen Finlay with Peter Williams and Christine Whitehead 'Evaluation of the Help to Buy Equity Loan Scheme'.

34 The official evaluation does not discuss its own evidence that average prices of new homes bought with equity loans rose more steeply than those without, but it does note (p.22) that newly-built properties in the Midlands and the North of England may attract a greater premium than elsewhere. It is possible that this could account for this difference, although the premium would need to be hefty for this to be the case. Without data from the lower-price regions comparing the prices of newly-built properties purchased with and without equity loans, it is impossible finally to resolve this.

35 Shelter, 'How much help is help to buy?', Shelter Policy Library September 2015, p.3.

36 Shelter, 'How much help is help to buy?'. The estimate is based on an earlier calculation by the Planning and Housing Advice Unit that a 1 per cent increase in mortgage funding generates a 0.36 per cent rise in average house prices.

37 Christian Hilber and Olivier Scöni, 'On the unintended consequences of housing policies' LSE Spatial Economics Research *Centre*, 18 January 2016.

38 Brian Green, 'Is George's housing prescription simply a marvellous medicine to boost home ownership?', *Brickonomics*, 27 November 2015: http://brickonomics.building.co.uk/2015/11/is-georges-housing-prescription-simply-a-marvelous-medicine-to-boost-home-ownership/.

39 'Through the roof', *The Spectator*, 9 January 2016.

40 Simon French, 'The Help to Buy ISA is economic illiteracy laid bare'.

41   ' Help to Buy: MPs question £10bn cost and impact on housing shortage', *The Guardian*, 18 June 2014.

Chapter 7 – Some modest proposals

1   Martin Wolf, 'Britain's self-perpetuating property racket', *Financial Times*, 8 January 2015.

2   Ben Pattison with Diane Diacon and Jim Vine, 'Tenure Trends in the UK Housing System', Building and Social Housing Foundation, 2010.

3   In 2009, the Labour government housing minister, John Healey, told the Fabian Society that the decline of owner occupation 'may not be such a bad thing,' while the Scottish minister for housing, Alex Neil, spoke of the need 'to challenge the culture with the obsession of home ownership.' Both are quoted in Ben Pattison with Diane Diacon and Jim Vine, 'Tenure Trends in the UK Housing System', p.28.

4   'Boosting home ownership should not be a policy aim in its own right. The government's aim should be to improve affordability in general', Kristian Niemietz, 'The housing crisis: A briefing', Institute of Economic Affairs, March 2016, p.1.

5   Quoted in Christopher Hope, 'Thousands of new homes on green belt in biggest shake-up for 30 years', *Daily Telegraph*, 8 December 2015.

6   Centre for Policy Studies, 'What's behind the housing crisis?', Economic Bulletin 68, 20 November 2015. CML data quoted by Neal Hudson suggest that 64 per cent of those born in 1960 and 1970 owned their homes by age 35. For those born in 1980, the proportion was down to 44 per cent, and for those born in 1990 it is projected to be just 39 per cent ('The housing crisis: A crisis of home ownership?' Savills Housing Market Note 17 July 2015).

7   Bernard Clarke, 'Data shows housing tenure trends continuing' Council of Mortgage Lenders press release, 5 March 2015.

8   'Through the roof', *The Economist*, 26 September 2015.

9   Estimates by PwC, quoted in Kathryn Hopkins, 'Red hot market leaves Generation Rent out in cold' *The Times*, 17 November 2015.

10 Brian Green, 'Is George's housing prescription simply a marvellous medicine to boost home ownership?', *Brickonomics*, 27 November 2015: http://brickonomics.building.co.uk/2015 /11/is-georges-housing-prescription-simply-a-marvelous-medicine-to-boost-home-ownership/

11 An earlier Civitas report proposed ending overseas investment in residential property unless intended for personal use – see

David G. Green and Daniel Bentley, 'Finding Shelter', Civitas, 2014.

12 Australian non-nationals are only allowed to buy residential property if it adds to the housing stock (i.e. if they buy new, off-the-plan, or build themselves). David Green and Daniel Bentley ('Finding Shelter', Civitas 2014) propose Britain adopt the same policy, although the authors note that both the Chancellor of the Exchequer and the Mayor of London worry that any such a restriction might jeopardise the flow of overseas investment into London.

13 The 2008 crisis slashed the number of transactions, and the market has yet to recover from this. In 2007, there were 1.6m residential property sales in the UK, but this fell to just over 900,000 in 2008, and the number of sales did not recover to more than a million until 2013. In 2014 it was 1.2m. HMRC, 'UK property transaction statistics', November 2015, Table 5.

14 C.W./London, 'The strangest chart', *The Economist*, 24 September 2015.

15 For details year by year, see: http://www.stampdutyrates.co.uk/historic-rates.html

16 'The housing market: can we fix it?', *The Economist*, 16 January 2016. Ryan Bourne suggests that stamp duty should be scrapped altogether and that owners should be taxed instead on the imputed rental value of their homes, as they used to be before Schedule A tax was removed from owner-occupiers in the 1960s (Ryan Bourne, 'The UK doesn't need more social housing', *Daily Telegraph* 21 January 2016).

17 Bernard Clarke, 'Data shows housing tenure trends continuing' Council of Mortgage Lenders press release, 5 March 2015.

18 Daniel Chandler and Richard Disney, 'Housing market trends and recent policies', p.123.

19 Price Waterhouse Cooper, 'UK housing market outlook' In UK *Economic Outlook* July 2015. Giving Housing Association tenants the right to buy their homes has some obvious down-sides. It will reduce the size of the social rented sector, which is where most commentators think the greatest need is for new building. It will also bring more marginal owners into owner occupation (for councils and housing associations by definition provide rental housing for the least well-off sections of the population). These are the very people who will probably struggle most to repay their mortgages when interest rates finally rise.

20 'Jeremy Corbyn: Right to buy should be extended to private tenants' *Labour List*, 24 June 2015.

21 Daniel Bentley, 'The Future of Private Renting', Civitas, 2015.

22 'Renting families move so often they are nearly nomadic – new research' *Shelter Policy Blog*, 17 February 2016. The report claims 6 per cent of private renters had to change their children's school when they last moved home.

23 Anna Clarke, Sam Morris, Michael Oxley, Chihiro Udagawa and Peter Williams, 'The effects of rent controls on supply and markets', Cambridge Centre for Housing and Planning Research, May 2015.

24 Peter Rachman was a London landlord in the fifties and early sixties who became famous for the various unsavoury tactics he employed to get tenants out of his rent-controlled properties so he could sell or re-let at higher rents.

25 Labour Party, 'A Better Deal for Renters': http://www.labour.org.uk/issues/detail/renting

26 'Making tenancies family friendly', *Shelter Policy Blog*, 6 March 2014.

27 When first introduced in 1980, RTB discounts ranged between 33 per cent (for tenants of 3 years standing) and 50 per cent (after 20 years). In 1998, the Blair government tightened eligibility to 5 years tenancy and capped total discounts at £38,000 in London down to £22,000 in the north of England. These caps were further tightened in 2003 when discounts in areas of greatest housing need (most of London and the south-east) were reduced to £16,000. Sales dwindled to 3,000 pa by 2009/10. In 2012 the Coalition government raised the maximum discount to £75,000, and in 2013 the London maximum was raised to £100,000. Eligibility was also returned to the original 3 years. These maxima are now pegged to inflation. Currently, tenants in council houses who have been in occupation for 3 to 5 years qualify for a 35 per cent discount. After 5 years, the discount goes up by 1 per cent for every extra year of tenancy up to a maximum of 70 per cent, but this would not apply to private sector tenants whose TRB would expire at the end of a 5 year tenancy. Council tenants in flats get a discount after 3 years of 50 per cent, and this increases after 5 years by 2 per cent per annum up to the same maxima. Private sector tenants who buy flats would not be eligible for these higher rates. Details of the current scheme for council tenants can be found at: https://www.gov.uk/right-to-buy-buying-your-council-home/discounts. See also: Daniel Chandler and Richard Disney, 'Housing market trends and recent policies' and Wendy Wilson and Lizzie Blow, 'Extending home ownership – government initiatives', House of Commons Library , Standard Note SN/SP/3668,.20 March 2015

28 Hamptons International, 'The forecast issue' *Market Insight*, Autumn 2015, p.6.

29 Hamptons International, 'The forecast issue', p.5. In 2009 the Private Rented Sector initiative was launched to attract more institutional investors into rental housing. By 2016, the British Property Federation estimated that 30,000 build-to-rent homes were going through the planning system and that £30 billion of institutional investment was ready to go into housing over the next 5 years (Patrick Hosking, 'The Model T build-to-rent plan that may just solve our housing shortage', *The Times*, 2 March 2016). However, the attraction of investment in housing for many individual landlords is the capital gain rather than the income rate of return which, at an average of 3.3 to 3.6 per cent, is probably insufficient for most institutions to consider. Ben Pattison with Diane Diacon and Jim Vine, 'Tenure Trends in the UK Housing System', Building and Social Housing Foundation 2010.

30 Consideration might be given to extending this twenty-five year rule to sales across all housing tenures so that local authorities and housing associations know they can rely on a lengthy period of rental income when they put money into new housing developments.

31 For example, a landlord outside London owns a house valued at £400,000 which he/she bought 12 years ago for £200,000. The tenants have been in the property for between 3 and 5 years, which in principle entitles them to a 35 per cent discount, worth £140,000. However, the maximum discount is capped at £77,900 so the house is sold to them for £322,100. This gives the landlord a taxable capital gain of £122,100, but the tax concession proposed here would reduce this to £44,200. The CGT personal allowance is £11,100 (in 2015/16) with the balance taxable at 28 per cent for those in higher rates tax bands. The landlord in this example would therefore end up paying CGT of £9,268 – which still leaves a substantial post-tax capital gain on the original investment of £112,832. This can be compared with what would happen under current rules if the same landlord chose to sell at £400,000 (with no discount for the tenants). He/she would realise a taxable capital gain of £200,000, which would incur a CGT payment of £52,892, leaving a post-tax capital gain of £147,108.

32 Like any other business, the cost of borrowing should be deductible against tax on profits, but for BTL landlords, this was scrapped in 2015. It is sometimes argued that landlords should not be able to claim tax relief on mortgage interest payments given that home buyers can no longer do this, but owner-

occupied housing is not regarded by the tax system as a business asset, which is why it enjoys exemption from Capital Gains Tax. It is desirable that all businesses should be taxed in the same way on the same rules.

33 'We regularly hear that the solution to the housing crisis is to: relax planning, build on the green belt, provide mortgage guarantees, subsidise first-time buyer deposits, scrap stamp duty, levy a land value tax, build more council houses, tax the rich and so on. In reality, selecting an appropriate policy prescription to solve these interconnected but equally distinct problems is tough. Some policies may improve some problems, but make others worse. Furthermore short-term fixes may have nasty long-term effects... It's all a bit complicated' Brian Green, 'Is George's housing prescription simply a marvellous medicine to boost home ownership? *Brickonomics* 27 November 2015.

34 Angus Armstrong, 'Commentary: UK housing market problems and policies' *National Institute Economic Review* no.235, February 2016, F4-F8.

35 65 per cent of UK bank lending in 2012 was for residential mortgages with another 14 per cent for commercial real estate purchases. Only 14 per cent was for business investment other than real estate. Adair Turner, *Between Debt and the Devil*, Fig.4.1.

36 As Turner notes, different categories of credit have different elasticities of response to changing interest rates. A given rate rise might have next to no effect on the demand for housing loans if property prices are booming, yet it could cause severe harm for business investment. *Between Debt and the Devil* p.197.

37 Quoted by Nigel Keohane and Nida Broughton, 'The Politics of Housing', Social Market Foundation, 2014, p.43.

38 As Neal Hudson observes: 'The housing market crisis is closely interlinked with our low inflation, high debt economy... there is a clear tension between the desire of Government to increase home ownership and the need for the Bank of England to minimise future risks' (A crisis of home ownership? *Savills Housing Market Note*, 17 July 2015).

39 On manipulation of risk weightings, see Adair Turner, Between *Debt and the Devil*, p.202.

40 The Bank told lenders that no more than 15 per cent of loans should exceed four and a half times the borrower's income. Philip Aldrick, 'The Bank of England must take a measure of Carney's Canadian tonic', *The Times*, 6 February 2016.

41 *Between Debt and the Devil*, p.119.

42 Evidence from Sir John Cuncliffe to House of Lords Select Committee on Economic Affairs Inquiry on 'The Economics of the UK Housing Market', Session 11, 2 March 2016, transcript p.3.